even now

CLINGING TO WILD FAITH
IN THE MIDDLE OF YOUR STORY

verna bowman

© 2025 by Verna Bowman

Published by
Avodah Books
www.avodahbooks.com

ISBN 9781734778960 (paperback) | 9781734778977 (ebook)

All rights reserved. No part of this publication may be reproduced, stored in a retrieval system, or transmitted in any form or by any means—for example, electronic, photocopy, recording—without written permission of the publisher. The only exception is brief quotations in printed reviews.

All Scripture quotations, unless otherwise indicated, are from the New King James Version®. Copyright © 1982 by Thomas Nelson. Used by permission. All rights reserved. Scripture quotations marked NIV are from the Holy Bible, New International Version®, NIV®. Copyright ©1973, 1978, 1984, 2011 by Biblica, Inc.™ Used by permission of Zondervan. All rights reserved worldwide. www.zondervan.com. The "NIV" and "New International Version" are trademarks registered in the United States Patent and Trademark Office by Biblica, Inc.™ Scripture quotations marked ESV are from the ESV® Bible (The Holy Bible, English Standard Version®), copyright © 2001 by Crossway, a publishing ministry of Good News Publishers. Used by permission. All rights reserved. Scripture quotations marked NLT are from the Holy Bible, New Living Translation, copyright ©1996, 2004, 2015 by Tyndale House Foundation. Used by permission of Tyndale House Publishers, a Division of Tyndale House Ministries, Carol Stream, Illinois 60188. All rights reserved. Scripture quotations marked KJV are from the King James Version of the Bible. Public domain. Scripture quotations marked NASB1995 are from the (NASB®) New American Standard Bible®, Copyright © 1960, 1971, 1977, 1995 by The Lockman Foundation. Used by permission. All rights reserved. www.lockman.org. Scripture quotations marked NASB are from the (NASB®) New American Standard Bible®, Copyright © 1960, 1971, 1977, 1995, 2020 by The Lockman Foundation. Used by permission. All rights reserved. www.lockman.org. All emphasis in Scripture is the author's.

Cover design by Hannah Linder Designs
Cornfield image (page 187) by Sherise Rittenhouse

*To my amazing family
who taught me how to cling to wild faith.*

*Jesus, may You pour out Your spirit on every sweet soul
who picks up this book. Thank you for showing me
I could remain . . . even now.*

contents

prologue
1. the middle of redemption — 9
2. then this — 21
3. but now — 29

the middle
4. "up you get. you're fine." — 37
5. i don't remember me — 45
6. bible stories aren't just for kids — 53
7. those I met along the way — 57
8. what's your name—who's your daddy? — 69
9. seen and known — 77
10. on the days i can believe — 87
11. what if one line could tell your story? — 93
12. the middle of the stairwell — 97
13. when seasons change — 105
14. when you haven't got a prayer — 115
15. still yourself — 123
16. be the warrior — 131
17. the caller is the keeper — 139
18. soul mentoring — 145
19. it is well — 151
20. yet . . . i will — 157

epilogue
21. if you had a remembrance book — 165
22. embrace your story — 171
23. thus far — 177
    last thoughts — 181

notes — 183
acknowledgments — 185
about the author — 187

prologue

prologue

1
the middle of redemption

Salvation happens in a moment, but sanctification takes a lifetime. Because the lost need to be saved, the saved need to be healed, and the healed need to be mended.

VB

I was sitting in a church. I wasn't sure why. Wedged in the middle of the back pew, I wondered whether anyone would notice a pregnant me if I climbed over the few who were nodding out. I should have known I'd get trapped in the middle. Even though I was a church rookie, it didn't take long to see that the regulars staked their claim on each end. I was a stranger in a strange land and wanted to bolt — but I stayed.

The story of my life, hanging in when I wasn't sure if I could.

Back then, the few times I visited a church weren't anything I wanted to experience twice. It was fairly tortuous. This time was no different. I looked around at all the virtuous, wondering how many were just playing the part. It seemed like a pretentious Sunday morning show easily forgotten by Monday. Since I was with my children, I figured I'd simply sit it out unnoticed and get it over with. But that didn't happen.

Here's why . . .

While entertaining the thought of how to make a subtle exit, *instead* I went up to the front of the church to answer an altar call. *Front* of the church. *What?* And somebody looking the way I did back then standing at an altar rarely goes unnoticed. Only a God could make it happen.

I won't forget the day, no matter how many decades pass. It was an instant forever.

How could anything so dramatic happen to someone so set in her rebel ways? I walked in with a bad attitude, having immediately realized the church sign was a contradiction. I must have read it wrong. I didn't think *Come as you are* meant getting dressed up holy to look like somebody you aren't. I thought it meant *Come as* I *am*, not what you think I should be. And who knew that rawhide would clash with their idea of Sunday best? Besides, I've always been a denim kind of girl, so my idea of church clothes were jeans without too many revealing holes. I wouldn't have worn a hat, heels, and pearls if I got a prize.

If my children weren't enrolled in the school affiliated with the church, I wouldn't have been there at all. A mysterious God definitely has creative ways to get our attention, because having my kids part of a Christian school wasn't something I would have considered on my own. Especially after seeing that everyone was expected to play by their hallowed rules concerning hemlines and hairlines. It didn't take more than a minute to know I didn't want this place for me or my kids, believing there must be another way to keep them out of a Philadelphia public school.

Looking back, I can't entirely blame the church people. They had their ways, I had mine. And mine had walls. I was eager to help out at school events but opted out of the social part, finding it too uncomfortable to tolerate this crowd's Bible lingo. Every conversation was a verse. The few times I sat in on the church service, it turned into a lengthy sermon focusing on wrath, convincing me that my husband was going straight to hell because he wasn't there. And I was probably headed to the same place even though I *was* there. So it didn't sound like much of a win-win.

When the kids asked me to go to church with them, I'd usually sit in the parking lot and do my nails while they were in Sunday school. Honestly, I would have rather watched the grass grow than go inside. But over time something began to change as I continued to listen to my children recite their Scripture homework and read Bible stories, even though I wasn't on *the same page*.

I wasn't raised in a Christian home, so I wasn't even aware of the basics. Actually, it was a bit humbling when we read a story together one evening and my eight-year-old corrected me for mispronouncing a name. And small wonder—I still think it's phonetically ridiculous that Nebuchadnezzar isn't actually pronounced *Na-BUTCH-ad-nezzar*. So, when my son Tommy took over reading the rest of the story, he blew through the name *NEB-a-kid-nez-zar* like it was the kid next door. Turns out there was a golden statue of this guy ninety feet high somewhere and I'd never even heard of him.

Although I wasn't familiar with the Word of God, I heard it for the first time through the voice of my children. It wasn't long after the *Neb-fiasco* that they asked if I would please go *inside* the church with them. It just seems wicked to say no to a child who asks you to go to church.

So, I thought I'd give it another try if for no other reason than to learn how to pronounce silly names.

It was mid-September in 1975. As we drove to the church, I thought it would be just another dreaded service where I could get in and get out without anyone stopping to ask, "Where is your husband, when is your baby due, and are you washed in the blood?" I'm usually pretty quick with answers, but this last one threw me, so after some hesitation along with a wide-eyed stare, I stammered, "Uh . . . home in bed, March, and *what*?!"

Clearly, this wasn't the place for me.

But it turned out on this particular day, it was absolutely the place for me. I sat my wishing-I-was-invisible self down in the farthest seat I could find, discreetly nestled in between my ten-year-old daughter and eight-year-old son, wishing I was anywhere but in this church . . . in this pew . . . or on this planet.

Yes, I looked different so I stuck out, but I stuck it out. The story of my life. And it changed the story of my life.

The course of history was changed with two words, when Jesus called His disciples and said, "Follow Me." And so was the course of my history. If Christ would have asked me in that moment, "Verna, will you follow Me and will you remain?," my answer might have been a lot like the apostle Peter's hasty response: "Oh, absolutely!" Because we only see the moment. Somehow an invitation to follow doesn't sound as radical as remaining, especially throughout the harrowing journey that would be the backdrop of my life. Even so, my answer was a *yes*.

And still is.

Going is not knowing; going is trusting. And learning to trust hasn't come easy, so I'll take you back to the *pre-*

follow days to give a small example of how far away I once was . . .

And once were all of us.

This is where Jesus walked in. I had been married for twelve years, living in Philadelphia on the edge of Bucks County where I was raised. As our kids became school age, the last thing I wanted was to send them to a public school in the area, so I decided on a private school. A Christian private school sounded even better. Surprisingly, my rock-musician husband agreed, which was the first miracle because, like me, he expressed very little God-interest except for a "Now I lay me down to sleep" prayer at bedtime with the kids. We figured it was the classic childhood ritual following a bedtime story, sort of like "Goodnight, don't let the bedbugs bite."

By now, our marriage had been broken and semi-repaired so often that life became more desperate and dark than I realized. It must've been a huge transition for my kids to experience a Christian environment during the school day and the total opposite at home.

They were attending the school for only a few weeks when one agonizing day (and I've had countless) the pastor of the church and my son's teacher came for an unexpected visit. And I do mean *unexpected*.

Our house seemed to have a revolving door 24/7 with plenty of strange musician-visitors. The door was even strange. Our front door was covered in faux snakeskin. If I invited you in for a quick tour past the reptilian studded vinyl, you'd enter into an abode decorated in early-freak, everything black accented by trippy tapestry. Hippie floor-length beads hung in the doorways to separate bohemian-themed rooms. Our bedroom floor was a keep-you-up-at night zebra pattern surrounded by walls painted black featuring a gallery of posters from *Easy Rider*. And the weirdness extended to the downstairs family room where my husband kept his pet boa and python. You had to be there—but probably wouldn't want to be.

Neither did the visiting pastor and the schoolmarm who realized stopping by unannounced wasn't a good idea. However, one visit kept them from making the same mistake twice, because they never returned (I think they're still running).

The surprise visit came about while I was upstairs in the bathroom coloring my hair. When I heard a knock, I shouted down to whoever it was, "Just come on up!" They couldn't hear me and I could hardly hear them pounding on the snakeskin vinyl with the stereo belting out a deafening "Purple Haze," so I finally had to go down to answer the door. The gruesome-twosome appeared stuffed and mounted on the doorstep. They couldn't have looked more rigid unless they had been embalmed. The pastor was holding a huge Bible. I wondered, *What is he going to do with that?*

It's a good thing I'm shock-proof, although I wish they had been, since I wasn't wearing much more than the towel covering the sparkling-sherry-goop in my hair.

Reluctantly they came into the awkward setting but didn't seem like they wanted to stay. For. Some. Reason.

Maybe it was the patchouli.

I could tell right away they weren't Jimi Hendrix fans when they asked me to "turn down the awful music." I wasn't sure how to manage it without opening the lid to the stereo (consoles had lids in the Dark Ages). And inside the lid of our stereo was a nude picture of Janis Joplin covering a punch mark that went through the wood, from last night's battle. And keep in mind, I was wearing a towel.

The never-ending visit came to an abrupt close when my husband walked in. Since these two didn't appear like our *usual* visitors, he looked past them and asked me who they were and what they wanted. Maybe he thought the guy in the suit was a Bible salesman. Considering they both looked like they were baptized in vinegar, I didn't expect the conversation to last long. It began and ended with my husband saying, "I ain't buyin' what you're sellin', so see ya."

I'm certain this was when my face turned as sparkling-sherry as the hair dye. As I walked them to the door, he shouted for them not to let Warlock out—that was our cat. After they left (and eventually recovered), I'm guessing they spent most of their waking moments praying to get up enough nerve to return for an exorcism.

You can imagine how pleasantly stunned the pastor was when I responded to an altar call months later. I don't know how he didn't faint dead away. Unfortunately, it wasn't because of anything he said on that amazing day—in fact, it may have been in spite of what was said, because I remember hearing a lot of rules and regulations. I only know that during that *just as I am* moment I was moved in my heart to go forward no matter what was in the way. All these years later, I can remember the scent of the dear lady who prayed me into the kingdom when I went forward. Smelled like freedom.

And I knew, I didn't want to run and hide anymore. I wanted to kneel. And so I did.

Although everything changed, nothing changed. Something unexplainable and eternal happened, but when I got home the same sorry situation was still on the other side of the snakeskin door. I returned to an unfaithful marriage and criticism from skeptical family and friends. The peace I'd encountered collided with turmoil, and a battle over which would win had only just begun.

I continued to carry the weight of too much tie-dyed baggage to be able to look into a mirror without seeing deep scars. It took some time to become convinced that I was a new creation and that the old life was buried. I didn't feel new—altogether. I had no idea that faith wasn't about feelings. It was about grace. But I had to find out what that was.

But then . . .

> Therefore, if anyone is in Christ, he is a new creation. The old has passed away; behold, the new has come. (2 Corinthians 5:17 ESV)

It was hard for the people who knew me to believe that I could be anything but what they knew. With no Christian friends or family, I was on this trip alone. It was a challenge to search solo with so many unanswerable questions. There was no omniscient (all-knowing) Google back then, so I was totally dependent on the Holy Spirit. And I learned I could rely on Him.

Determined to find more of what I found, I became a church tramp, drifting from one church to another. I visited every flavor church there was in and around the metropolitan area. I just wanted a place to mend. A place to grow.

We all have to start somewhere, but *where?* It seemed a good starting place was to read the Bible and pray. But I didn't want to read the Bible and I didn't know how to pray.

The raw beginning was at the edge of a footstool. We had a black (of course) ottoman (some call it a hassock). Every morning at 7:15, after my husband left for his daytime job and my children left for school, I knelt at the ottoman. I foolishly thought that if I prayed at the same time, in the same place, the Lord might know where to look for me. Absurd, I know. But not for someone who was still trying to sort out if Noah built an ark just to mate his pets — and why, for heaven's sake?

The Father doesn't save us so we can coast through our conversion to stay the same.

The Father doesn't save us so we can coast through our conversion to stay the same. He accepts the *just as we are* to design a beauty. He will use whoever and whatever to bring it about. I am grateful for the *whoever* back then who had the kind sense to offer me a pocket testament instead of an over-my-head King James filled with a bunch of thees, thous, and shalt-nots. One of the first verses I came to was a promise:

Call upon Me in the day of trouble and I will rescue you, and you will honor Me. (Psalm 50:15 NASB)

The small book became a well-worn, dog-eared, marked-up treasure of pages bound by a tattered cover that held the voice of God inside. That little testament talked me through the pain of enduring a difficult pregnancy while my husband was involved with someone who was half my age. I was *twenty-eight*. Yes, you heard right.

So, I did call upon Him — and He did rescue me.

The immature prayers whispered alongside a black ottoman were tearful hopes for a marriage and family to somehow be mended. It wasn't. When my husband left six weeks after our third child was born, I watched from the doorway longer than I needed to. As the trace of him faded from my life along with the taillights into the night, I felt abandoned by him and by God. I unwittingly thought I must not be a very good pray-er.

Later—much later—I recognized how God's good answer of protection and rescue came out of those unanswered prayers. Even then in my small faith, I knew I had no ground on which to approach God other than His grace and mercy. He saved me from a bizarre life that took some time to get over, long after getting over it. And some of you know exactly what that means. Most all of us can see in the rearview that there's always something we wish could have turned out differently.

And so, I was a divorced single mom in my twenties. And God was still sovereign and God was still good. And God was just as sovereign when I remarried the following year, but it was only the beginning of many more devastating middles.

I share my early days because I've been asked several times through the years, "How did you get from *so far there* to *so far here* and remain faithful in the hard middle?"

That's a question for all of us, and this book is my answer.

> *Being confident of this, He who began a good work*
> *in (your name) will carry it on to completion*
> *until the day of Christ.*
> *(from Philippians 1:6)*

pause in the middle

Dear friend, how did you get from *so far there* to *so far here* and remain faithful in the hard middle?

2
then this

No matter our past, no matter our now, through the unexplained grace and power of Jesus we can be transformed into a new beginning.

VB

My mom loved putting puzzles together. She was patient and detailed while adding each piece in place, but there were times she fumbled and mumbled through the spread-out mess that wasn't even close to the picture on the box. She was right about more than an unassembled puzzle when she pointed out, "You think this will be easy after the corners are in place, but then you look at the scrambled middle and you're ready to give up."

So much like life.

I thought a new beginning should look more like the corners were in place, more like *my* picture on the box—but too many pieces were still missing.

It seemed impossible to sort through a newfound faith in the emotional mix of postpartum and divorce, and even crazier to expect the kids to understand something that I couldn't. They were struggling between the hurt and excitement of having their new baby brother come home to a broken family. It was during this time when I learned to wear my *I'm fine* mask more often in hopes they'd believe that they could be fine too. But behind the mask, I couldn't imagine how life could work for a single stay-at-home mom with three littles in the mid-'70s. My only assurance came from the sound of the kids' laughter in make-believe places and the sweet contentment of a nursing baby who didn't have any idea of what it meant to be abandoned.

As I was trying to process whether life was falling apart or falling together, it became more complicated when I received a call from an old acquaintance. Up until then I had been avoiding the fair-weather friends who seemed to know more of what had gone on in my life than I did. If I told you just a little, you'd think I was exaggerating, so we'll skip it. I couldn't take any more bizarre *reality*. It was too painful.

I wondered how a trivial amount of faith could hold an unraveled mess together. For years it was like living in a fishbowl since we were somewhat in the public eye. Everyone knew the dirt. So, it didn't come as a surprise when this once-familiar guy called to say he heard through the grapevine about my situation. After experiencing countless betrayals and fake friendships, I hesitated when he asked if he could come to visit. I doubted whether I would ever trust again. I even doubted Mr. Rogers when he said it was a beautiful day in the neighborhood.

And I had my doubts about how faithful God would be.

But for the moment, I was glad to get a call from Jeff since I remembered him to be one of the good guys. *Sort of* glad. Even though he showed up at the right time, I remained cautious. Since there was a past connection with him to mutual friends in the band, I didn't feel comfortable until I was sure he had little contact with them. Gradually, I relaxed my guard when I sensed his genuine concern for my children.

One of the things that sold me on Jeff was shortly after we started seeing one another, he wanted to include the children and asked all of us out to dinner. Obviously, this guy never had any kids, because one of our early dates was an intimate dinner for five. It definitely didn't add to a romantic atmosphere when the baby shot out a ripe diaper (complete with sound effects) and slowly slid through the highchair onto the floor while the other two were deciding whether they wanted to order lobster. I thought he'd never look back once he dropped us off, but the kind of person he was at that time was the kind of dad he became — selfless.

Jeff filled in the missing pieces and fit right into the corners of our puzzle. So, the following year I asked the kids, "Should we marry him?" They were thrilled, and we celebrated our decision with a beautiful May wedding. We all said, "I do."

I should've remembered that after saying "I do," life changes. A lot.

We tried to make our own changes at first. We sold our homes in Philadelphia to start over by relocating far enough from the familiar tribe that was still at my door. Although the small town of Chalfont was only an hour away, it seemed like a private planet compared to the fishbowl life I had been living for so long.

However, not long after we were pronounced a *happily ever after*, our honeymoon was interrupted with a heart-shattering phone call. The emotionless voice on the other end almost sounded like an automated call: "I'm Dr. Someone from Somewhere calling for your mother who is too upset to come to the phone. Your father has been diagnosed with terminal cancer and she needs you here." A quick-and-done death sentence that didn't insert any other words or feeling than what I've just written. Needless to say, the honeymoon was over.

I had been aware something was seriously wrong for weeks. Especially when my dad wasn't strong enough to come to the wedding. He was a tall man with a sturdy frame from working hard over the years, so I was shocked to hear that my invincible dad, the strongest man I knew, was dying. And I had to find out in this way—at this time.

Jeff and I immediately returned home and made arrangements for my dad to live with us so that my mother could continue working. She came to stay with us on weekends. Six weeks later, he was gone and I was beyond devastated. It was hard to have the joy of a bride while consoling my mom who was now a grieving widow. Our new family had to adapt quickly to many obstacles—especially the kids who were still reeling from a broken home, a new stepdad, relocating to a new area, and grieving the loss of a beloved grandparent. Our family learned early on to live with interruptions in the middle of the story—together.

That's why it was God-sent to find a little Bible-preaching church right down the road from our new home. For months, I had been tramping around different churches near Philly, but this little country church was warm and genuine and the people were unlike the starched saints from before. The congregation was tender and real, and I looked forward to going every Sunday. Jeff not so much. He usually stayed home to do chores or made other excuses not to go. He respected my beliefs but didn't have many of his own at that time. Being raised in Girard College, an orphanage for fatherless boys, didn't give Jeff exposure to anything concerning faith since clergy were barred from campus.

So, with me going solo again, it didn't take long before a sour lady with a face tighter than her bun noticed me sitting husbandless with a bunch of kids and leaned over the pew one morning to ask if I was "unevenly yoked." I turned and said, "Probably. What's a yoke?"

I guess every church has one (or a dozen-ish) of these, but I couldn't help wondering whether she followed me from the church in Bensalem. I thought of responding with a "judge not lest ye be judged," but I was fairly new at this and wasn't sure if I had it right. I heard Harriet Oleson say it once on *Little House on the Prairie*, but then Pa Ingalls corrected her.

Up until this point, my short journey seemed more like a faith-crawl than a faith-walk, but when we got up on our four feet I realized that God must have brought Jeff and I together for a bigger plan than ours.

Time proved it true, but we soon found there was more to the *I do* than we were ready for.

God used the first year we were married to grow us up and grow us together to prepare our family for what was to come. We were seriously slammed with one incident after another. I was certain at the time, and even more so now as I look back, that the Lord brought us to this little church in Chalfont *for such a time as then*. It's where Jeff eventually dedicated himself to the Lord. Afterward, I was hoping to come across the tighter-than-her-bun-lady again, now that I was officially "evenly yoked." But I never saw her again.

Right in the middle between the vows and our first anniversary, *then this* . . .

Shortly after the shock of losing my dad, others followed

too quickly. Two of my close friends, both young and with families, suddenly died. One was the drummer in my ex-husband's band. The other was the father of the teenage girl who was the reason that my ex-husband left our marriage. A few months later, my eighteen-month-old son Shane was diagnosed with a rare condition and nearly died. I remained with him day and night until I was so weak from the stress that it resulted in a miscarriage of an early pregnancy. Then Jeff lost his business.

Simply listing a litany of tragic events couldn't possibly describe the anguish and questions in between the lines of what seemed to be the longest year ever. I felt like I was in an enemy war zone. *And I was*. It grew me up strong and fast as I discovered that every story has a hard and sacred middle that will either draw us closer to or turn us farther away from our God.

This first intense year could have destroyed what little faith I was holding on to while spinning out in spiritual vertigo, wondering if *returning to the Egypt* of my old life would be such a bad idea. Yes, my past had been a wreck, but this seemed worse. I can't be the first to feel that way. Nothing made sense. I guess it's easy to get drawn back to our old life, no matter how enslaving it seemed, when we're over the top in overwhelm.

Only grace prevents making a U-turn.

The twelve years of enduring a toxic marriage was a lot to move on from, but after coming out of the pain only to collide with twelve months of more pain in my new marriage stopped me in my tracks. The soul-shaking events that made up one calendar year set in place firm edges of the puzzle. Now I had to learn to trust God with the rest of the pieces that didn't fit yet.

When my baby son Shane nearly died, it did something

that took my faith to a place I never thought I'd go. It was the first huge step I took toward a loving Father who was teaching me to walk in strong shoes. In the grieving moments when I thought I couldn't take another step, I begged God's will to align with a mother's heart. But it was in this dark season I learned to beg a mother's heart to align with God's will.

In the grieving moments when I thought I couldn't take another step, I begged God's will to align with a mother's heart. But it was in this dark season I learned to beg a mother's heart to align with God's will.

I've had to relearn this hard truth countless times after another son was born. I needed to do more than trust and believe. I needed to trust and believe for a miracle. And I need one now.

And that's when I started to learn that the more we trust God, the more we entrust to God.

Remember the former days, _____, when after being enlightened you endured a great conflict of suffering.
(from Hebrews 10:32)

pause in the middle

Dear friend, what do you need to entrust to God?

3
but now

She stopped in the middle of the story and measured God. A deeper faith waits until the end of the story and interprets experience through the lens of God's faithfulness.

PAUL MILLER, *A LOVING LIFE*

How often have you stopped in the middle of your story to measure God through the cracked lens of brokenness, wondering if He is enough? It happens. We seem to believe God can part seas until we're the one struggling in the deep.

After a difficult first year of marriage, Jeff and I were crazy with excitement when our baby was about to be born and add to the blessing of our ready-made family. Although Jeff sincerely became a real dad when he adopted my children into his heart, he had been anticipating his own bio-baby for a long time. After two failed marriages, finally at forty years old he became a dad for the first time.

But then . . .

Joy was overshadowed with sorrow on the day baby

Geoff was born with kidney failure and immediately taken from us to be airlifted to an inner-city hospital. When forever changes quickly, it's hard to keep up.

It happened without warning. It always does.

Babies should come with a warning label: *This child will change your life.* I think all kids change our lives. But this baby taught me more than I ever thought I could learn.

The frigid January day began like any other, but could have ended horribly different if I hadn't gone to the hospital in the exact moment. And there was no reason to go, except for an unsettled gnawing within me. After three children and multiple miscarriages, I was definitely familiar with labor. However, this time there were no symptoms of labor and the baby wasn't due until the following month. And yet I felt the unexplained urgency to go to the hospital twenty miles away in the middle of a snowstorm. I didn't want an unnecessary wild goose chase for Jeff, but after praying with my daughter, I asked to go to the hospital. *Now.*

Upon arrival, following tests and chaos, I was rushed to the delivery room. Later that day after our baby was born, I was told that I arrived within a half hour of our son being stillborn.

Thirty minutes.

Words fail to describe the desperation of a mother helplessly lying in a sterile room while hearing the sound of a helicopter take flight with what has just been stolen from her womb. A hemorrhage and endless tears were all I had to show that my baby had been within me. I felt powerless having to remain in a suburban hospital far from a cry I could almost hear from forty miles away. Daily negative reports from the doctors only made it louder. And echo. But nothing they said could be heard over the voice in the night when a loving Lord whispered assurance from the Gospel pages of John: "This illness is not unto death, but for the glory of God" (11:4).

The first verse of Scripture I ever knew I owned. I read it, I heard it, it was mine. And I knew I would hold onto it for the rest of my life. And his.

The *then this* has been a long time from the *but now*. Time seems to have stood still in the lingering middle of an arduous forty-plus-year journey as we wait for another life-saving kidney transplant, since my son rejected his fourth in the spring of 2020. A quarantine turned a month-long hospital stay into a pandemic-prison with no one permitted to go inside. This is when I sat down with a pen and began writing this book. *Longhand*. I feel as limited today as I write this as back in the *but then*.

It's unfathomable how we were kept apart then, and we were kept apart again in this desperate moment. At the time of his birth, I couldn't get to the hospital where he was transferred due to an impossible snowstorm that immobilized the city. Now decades later, as he was near death, I was unable to get into the hospital due to a relentless virus immobilizing the world. We think we have control—until we don't.

Experience and age teach me every day that I'm not in control of anything other than to believe in the One who is.

When I stop in the middle of this long story to measure God, I can only measure myself. Who can span omnipotence or explain sovereignty? Not one of us. We only need to look between the lines of our stories to find the sacred measure of who *we* are. So, through the years when I've attempted to answer the question of how I got so far from *there* to *here* with the never-ending battle in between, it's as immeasurable as the One who writes our story with His glory. The infinite One who is able to take a faithless rebel and use every grueling chapter to grow her into a woman with a tenacious faith who will stand at the foot of a mountain and say, "Move!"

All it takes to behold a miracle is to see God do something only He can do. Jesus told His disciples if they had a speck of mustard-seed faith, it would be enough to make a mountain move. The way I understand it is how every circumstance seems to grow the seed a little more to level the massive things we face.

A pile of life has happened since I walked down the aisle with Jesus so long ago, but I learned early on that there is a greater depth of knowing God than being saved. The mystery of mercy had my older children bring me to Jesus through placing them in a Christian school when I was content to be a heathen. My younger children were instrumental in building my faith and keeping me close. And all four have taught me how to believe in miracles.

Jesus is a good Savior who knows the way to His Father's house. We only need to *follow*.

Jesus is a good Savior who knows the way to His Father's house. We only need to *follow*.

I hope by sharing these early pieces of my life, it will reassure you that none of us are too far from His holy reach no matter how dark our past, no matter how bleak our circumstances. God is faithful and deserves more than a fickle faith that caves when we feel He has failed us because things go wrong.

And they will.

You can probably tell, I'm not about the polish and pomp of writing styles and guidelines to do it a certain way with a must-have platform. My journal and pen are my platform. My reason to string sentences together in blogs that become books is to reach those who are hurting and need encouragement. I could have written a few sequels after writing my first book, with all that has poured out on life within that time, but I'm writing just this one that took so long.

Even now. For you.

*The Lord is close to the brokenhearted
and saves _____ who is crushed in spirit.
(from Psalm 34:18)*

pause in the middle

In the middle of what crushing circumstances have you wondered if God is enough?

the middle

4
"up you get. you're fine."

> *Our greatest glory is not in never failing*
> *but in rising up every time we fail.*
> RALPH WALDO EMERSON

Why is it when so many people are hurting, they say they're just fine? I'm sure you have been asked countless times how you're doing and responded with a hasty and untrue "I'm fine." Me too. (I lie to myself, but I don't believe me.) It seems to be a standard greeting with an automatic answer. But sooner or later, we should deal with what's hidden behind the auto-response. If I had a therapist, I'm sure they'd agree.

What you've read so far tells of a life that was far from fine. And yet, I was determined to die laughing even if I felt killed by circumstances. I've spent a lot of life pretending to be fine and proving to myself that I am. Whether pretending or proving, it's an unhealthy way to process. And it's taken years to become soul-honest.

As a young girl, I told myself my dad was just a heavy

drinker until I was able to define it as alcoholism. As a young wife, I believed things could change in a grossly unfaithful marriage until I found out too late that they never would. And throughout the painful chapters that make up life, it became a pattern for me to tell myself a better story.

I was diagnosed with rheumatoid arthritis (RA) decades ago. Since RA radically influences everyday life and mood, I've been groomed to fake okay. When I'm experiencing a flare, even squeezing a tube of toothpaste or holding a coffee cup can be an extremely difficult task. But *I'm fine.*

Three out of three sons have nearly died, and my husband came close to death at least four times over the years before he actually passed. But *I'm fine.*

Pretending to be fine is more painful when you get good at it. And I did.

So, when did this pretending begin and why did it continue? I had to know. It's a question for all of us who aren't allowing ourselves to *not* be fine. Especially for Christians, we believe we should be *happy, happy, happy* because *we have the joy, joy, joy* all the time. If that was so, there wouldn't be so many examples of Bible giants with such a range of lamenting emotions.

So, when I try to get to the root of why it's easier to sweep the piled-high dirt under the rug, I look back to yesteryear. A lot of what shapes our adult selves is hidden in our childhood experiences.

Let's look there . . .

I was twelve years old. Once a week, my mom sent me to the spring for water. This was back in the age of no Fiji, when water was free. I'm still not sure why we needed spring water when we had a well, but oh well. Off I'd go with a half-dozen glass bottles in my bicycle basket, up or down the steep gravel hill of Sycamore Ave. It doesn't sound safe—and it wasn't. Glass and gravel never mix. Especially if you're showing off.

One afternoon, my close friend Mary and I rode our bikes from the spring with our baskets filled with the bottles, and on the way home I foolishly started racing her coming down the hill. Yep, you saw it coming. I skidded sideways on the loose gravel and was thrown over the handlebars. And the glass caught up.

Mary helped a broken me and a broken bike get back home. My dad pulled up from work just as my chronic-worrier mom was wringing her hands and trying to pick shards out of torn flesh. I wasn't sure which one of us was going to black out first, but I figured it would be me since all I could see were multiple stars floating in the darkness.

I whispered, "Mom, I think I'm blind. Don't tell Dad."

"Well, of course he's going to know, Verna," she nervously burst out.

Wow. Just wow. I was hoping for a little reassurance from dear old mom, like, "Don't be silly! Of course you're not blind!" The sadly absurd "don't tell Dad I'm blind" says it all. From the time I was a kid, it was about being broken and trying to keep it from being known. Even from those closest to me.

And it defined my life for a long time because I thought I could control my wounds by denying them. It didn't matter how busted up in life I became as long as I could keep it from others. I see this little scene as the beginning of not honestly owning my story, believing if no one could see the struggle, then it must not be real.

Here's another example . . .

I was close to my paternal grandmother and loved spending time with her. She wasn't a warm-fuzzy, but she was mine. And she was a huge influence to encourage me to be strong from a young age. Emily Rose had experienced much hardship in her life. She was a strong, hard-working, salty old Irish woman who didn't mince words. She didn't hug. If I fell down, the only comfort she offered was, "Up you get. You're fine."

Born in steerage on a ship coming from Ireland, she married teenage-young and raised her tough brood of eight kids in Kensington, a rough part of Philadelphia. Sadly, she lost a few of her children—stillborn twins, a five-year-old boy, and a son in the war. After she raised her family, she moved to a modest house on a few acres in Bucks County.

She had a gift for gardening. Her unassuming little home had a greenhouse, and the grounds were smothered in flowers and vegetable gardens. This lady had two green thumbs. She could throw corn seeds on the sidewalk in the morning and have stalks growing in the cracks by dinner. Every picture I have of Grandma Rose has her wearing an old straw hat, holding a rake in one hand and a metal watering can in the other. I still have that battered old watering can proudly displayed on my front porch. It's useless and rusted, filled only with holes. Although it no longer holds water, it remains a treasure that pours out her stories. And they never run out.

Her interesting tales were as varied as the sweet fragrance of her roses, nestled alongside the foul-smelling boxwood (which has the scent of an unneutered cat). I loved our garden chats until she had me weed, hoe, and rake. The times I whined about the thorns, bugs, bees, and a slithering snake, she'd wipe her face with her apron, peer over her sweaty spectacles, and sternly remark, "Silence yourself! You have to learn to stand strong no matter what comes near."

Grandma Rose would grip my forearm and lead me to

the edge of the garden and point out the tall flowers that stood strong. Then she had me look over to the ones that wilted easily, as she stated with a slight Gaelic lilt,

Flowers tell a story ~
Some remain tall and stately and can face hard seasons.
Some don't hold up; they wither and get wilted by life.
You need to decide which one you will be, Verna Rose.

And I did decide.

My grandmother wasn't a woman of faith, but she was preaching wise words that would actually help me through a life that didn't turn out easy. Words I remember to this day. But Grandma's garden boot camp was good training that worked until it didn't, because we're only as strong as *us* without God.

We're only as strong as *us* without God.

We need more than our own effort to bounce back from heartbreak and tragedy. We need something beyond our limited power. These words have been a pillar for me to lean on over and over: "I can do all things through Him who strengthens me" (Philippians 4:13 NASB).

Think of how this is true in your story—in the valleys of shadows that you could never have walked through without God's strength. Think of the past experiences that help you to realize how they have shaped you.

Dear one, how can we learn to *feel our feelings* instead of "Up you get. You're fine"?

One answer for me has been to keep a journal, a safe place to recognize and store my feelings. The most important lesson that journaling teaches is authenticity. Whether we're fine or we're not, our page will shed honest light between the lines. Real life is a constant battle to keep real. But simple truth-telling helps us connect more deeply with our Father, with ourselves, and with others.

Recently, I appreciated this bare and raw response from a Christian friend on a not-so-fine day concerning a serious matter in her family. I asked how she was doing and she simply said, "I know what I know, but I'm scared." That meant she knew to trust God in her situation but honestly she was unsure in the moment. And haven't all of us experienced the unsure moments?

I'm curious how we'd respond if God asked us how we're doing today or in this particular season of life. If we came back with the auto-reply "Just fine," He'd be out of a holy job.

The Lord is _____'s strength and _____'s shield.
In Him my heart trusts and I am helped.
My heart exults and with my song I give thanks to him.
(from Psalm 28:7)

verna bowman

pause in the middle

How are you—really?

5
i don't remember me

I know who I was when I got up this morning,
but I think I must've been changed several times since then.
LEWIS CARROLL, *ALICE'S ADVENTURES IN WONDERLAND*

When the new me collided with the old me, it had me curious of who I had been and who I was becoming. And who I was in this moment. Salvation may be a quick and radical re-do, but sanctification is a slow makeover that can hurt. Some days I would grow. Some days I would shrink. Trials can do that to a girl. But like Alice, bewildered in Wonderland, I was trying to make sense out of the nonsense.

One thing that was clear was Alice's uncertainty when the caterpillar asked, "Who are *you*?," I could have said right along with her, "I hardly know. . . . I can't explain myself . . . because I'm not myself, you know."[1]

I can't explain myself, but it's like this . . .

I was one way one minute and different in another, and the only thing in the middle of the minute was Jesus. I was undone by a love that chased a reckless teenager and then continued to chase a wayward adult for longer than a minute. Faithfully.

And He knew I didn't like her. But He loved her.

I know what it is to be smitten with too much world. And it's not there. I was good at being lost but didn't think I could be good at being saved. Only Jesus can make that sentence beautiful.

My maiden name was Rose, but I wrecked it. Then I got married and received a second name and it nearly wrecked me. So I told myself a Rose by any other name would smell as sweet. Shakespeare made the point long before I did that the names of things do not affect what they really are. However, when I was reborn and renamed Verna Bowman, it definitely affected me. And I liked her.

I find it hard to remember the twenty-eight-ish person who looked, talked, thought, and behaved so differently than the version that is now nearly fifty years older. And all these years later, I remain awestruck that grace and mercy was all it took.

However, I struggled in between the names, dealing with the overflow of baggage. The heavy burdens and unwanted memories were weighing me down, and that created an unwanted attitude to continually shield myself with self-protection. It can slow down the pace of transformation when we refuse our freedom in Christ. And it did, at first. If I'm honest, I still have to be on guard not to always be on guard.

When we recognize that being transformed means we aren't in charge of the change, it's freeing. Certainly we have a role in it, but it is the work of the Holy Spirit. We're not saved by changing our lives; our lives are changed by being saved. It's important to be mindful that God doesn't redeem us through the blood of Jesus so we can feel like constant failures.

God doesn't redeem us through the blood of Jesus so we can feel like constant failures.

We are prone to beat ourselves up when we don't grow at the speed of light, instead of letting grace and growth happen by just faithfully following. I have spoken to many who lose heart, thinking they will never get it right, and turn away. Please don't. You're not alone.

Many of us aren't even aware that we're walking around with an invisible backpack that can make us believe the lie. It weighs us down with the heaviness of never measuring up because of the times we carry anger, anxiety, fear, and rejection even though the divine and the agony already paid the price. Now that I mention it, maybe you notice it.

What if we had to wait to get to heaven to finally throw down this unbearable sack at the feet of Jesus and hear Him say with a holy sigh, "Why'd you bring the bag? I told you I took care of it."

To all the weary, Jesus says, "Come, you who are heavy laden. Take my yoke upon you" (see Matthew 11:28–30). He promises rest and true restoration. We read the words, but seem to yoke up till the next hard moment takes us down. There is no way for us to carry the heaviness that surrounds us today, adding to the crushing weight of what is expected of us every day.

I'm sure you can relate. There are times when my identity has been so scrambled I didn't know whose story I belonged to. I somehow vanished from my own story while being needed in everyone else's. It can happen. Our misplaced self tries to be *all*—the loving daughter, devoted wife, caring mother, fun-loving gramma, dependable caregiver, ministry leader, or fill in your own countless blanks. Even though the multidimensional *us* remains long after the role may change, can we find the girl who is somewhere inside?

Maybe you have been on the same path hoping to meet up with *you* again after being written into the stories of so many throughout your life. As women, we experience the demand of wearing multiple hats that make up the backdrop of our cluttered lives. So, like Alice, it's easy to fumble for the simple answer when we're asked who we are. But no matter where we've been or what we've been through, we get to decide where we go from here.

A huge weight was lifted when I no longer allowed humans to draw the line to tell me who I was, wasn't, or should be. Jesus is a good Savior. He died for all of it. When everyday logic makes no more sense than Alice's journey chasing a white rabbit, I'll decide where it goes from *here* and intentionally be a God-chaser, especially when it doesn't make sense. Even when it feels like we're shrinking, we're actually growing through the transformation. Go ask Alice when she's ten feet tall.

Yes, there have been times when I go past familiar places from wilder days and I can vaguely see the girl who once resided in my flesh. *That one.* I don't often revisit her, because I'd rather look back even further to remember the young girl who skipped through wildflowers and didn't see weeds. The girl who read fairy tales and believed they would come true. And the girl who made wishes on stars dancing above her. *That one.*

Can you remember the girl in you who saw things better than they were even if they weren't?

It reminds me of the John Lennon lyric about life being

what happens to us while we're busy making other plans. And then along the way we begin to notice the weeds, the fairy tale is just a tale, and the stars go dim. Because we notice the not-so-good.

It's easy to fall into despair as it grows darker on this planet. I talk with countless women of strong faith who are fighting for a fresh perspective to look at the brighter part, but it's more and more difficult with media overload turning down the lights. If we're not careful, we can get caught up with every wind and doctrine, measure ourselves by unrealistic standards, and get overcome with senseless strive and stress. We need to continually remind ourselves of who we are and not lose sight of what God has not only taken us *out of* but what He has brought us *to*.

When you become your best critic and your best isn't good enough, remember that God uses our failures. The Bible says not one of us is good enough but the cross of Jesus changes our status. Read Ephesians 2:1–10 and you'll find that not being good enough is exactly what qualifies us for His mercy.

Every one of us has a past without Christ. Obviously. So then, every one of us needs a Savior.

It's not that we weren't just *not okay*. We were dead. If God's Word tells us that we are loved and made righteous through Him, that should be validation enough. You'd think.

> But God, being rich in mercy, because of His great love which He loved us, even when we were dead in our wrongdoings, made us alive together with Christ (by grace you have been saved). (Ephesians 2:4–5 NASB)

Thinking of the *good enough* reminds me of a sweet girl I went to elementary school with who was oh-so-good. Her name was Susie. She had freckles and ribbons in her pigtails. She wore pinafores and patent-leather Mary Jane shoes, and she could skip rope to a hundred. She always won the spelling bee. She seemed perfectly-good.

However, in middle school Susie had to go away because she got "in trouble" (an antique expression from back in the day meaning having a baby out of wedlock). It happened. It was the age of innocence before we were pummeled with too much information. Hard to understand, but even the pigtailed Susies of the world are of the world. The world is *us* before Jesus.

We all make mistakes and have regrets, but how liberating to know that we can move forward in repentance and confidence knowing it is wiped away if we are a child of God.

So, if you are—remember who you *were*. So you won't forget who you *are*. Because the enemy repeatedly tries to remind you who you *aren't*.

Say it again.

I don't want to totally forget the me I was before Jesus, because it tells who He is in me now. Jesus doesn't make us *better*; He makes us *new*.

And if that's true for you, this is you . . .

- I am *complete* in Him. (Colossians 2:10)
- I am *alive* with Christ. (Ephesians 2:5)
- I am *holy* and without blame before Him in love. (Ephesians 1:4)
- I am *born of God*, and the evil one does not touch me. (1 John 5:15)
- I am *forgiven* of all my sins. (Ephesians 1:7)

- I am *redeemed* from the curse of sin. (Galatians 3:13)
- I am a *believer* and the light shines in my mind. (2 Corinthians 4:4)
- I am *free* from the law of sin and death. (Romans 8:2)
- I am His *workmanship*. (Ephesians 2:10)
- I am *greatly loved* by God. (Romans 1:7)
- I am *delivered* from the power of darkness. (Colossians 3:13)

And I am sure of this, that He who began a good work in _____ will bring it to completion at the day of Jesus Christ.
(from Philippians 1:6)

pause in the middle

Do you struggle with your identity in Christ or doubt who you are because of what others think of or expect of you?

6
bible stories aren't just for kids

A little faith will bring your soul to heaven; a great faith will bring heaven to your soul.
CHARLES SPURGEON

Do you remember learning to walk? Neither do I. Neither do any of us. It just happened by way of baby steps made up of falls and bumps that eventually took us somewhere. It's the same with our faith walk—the place of small beginnings.

A small step but giant leap for me was way back in the day when I stopped by a neighborhood Vacation Bible School with my kids. It was mid-summer, the kids were bored, and the church was offering VBS for the week, so I thought I'd drop off my younger boys. But then I decided to stay one morning to be a helper since my teens volunteered with the crafts. I knew right after making dried noodle necklaces and singing a few stanzas of "Father Abraham," I wanted to go back the next day. As a *mom*.

Looking back through the lens of simpler times, I see a

even now

teacher reading from an old holy book that left a mark that never faded. We met in the corner room in the old cinderblock wing of the church. It smelled like paste and oatmeal cookies. The cracks in the walls were covered with posters of Bible-story heroes—most were unfamiliar to me (I was a Bible rookie). The beautiful one that stood out was of a gentle Jesus knocking at the door.

That week I noticed little souls being molded while building popsicle-stick arks and making construction-paper crosses. My soul became molded right along with theirs as the Bible came to life with people wearing the same flesh and fear as me. Before then, I figured only super-saintly brave and unflawed giant slayers and those who parted water got featured stories.

Old Mrs. Landis knew the Bible like the back of her wrinkled hand. She sat with the children under a shade tree in the churchyard. It looked like a scene from the *Little House on the Prairie* set. Sounds archaic, but a Bible and the flannelgraph images of Daniel, Noah, and Moses were the only tools she needed to take you there—to hear the growl in the den, the smell in the ark, and feel the heat from the burning bush. No need for techie theatrics and drama.

Thankfully, Mrs. Landis welcomed an adult woman of small faith to eavesdrop on lessons that I thought were meant for kids. Her gift of sharing the heartbeat of regular people who preserved and experienced miracles, trials, and victories made it honest because every one of them had an untold middle. Like we do. And their yesteryear stories were written to encourage those of us today to survive the current times. Cover to cover, the Bible is made up of stories that help us get to the other side of our own.

The Bible is made up of stories that help us get to the other side of our own.

Years after Adam and Eve's fall in the garden of Eden, God carried out His plan to redeem humanity with a man named Abraham. If you haven't already, go ahead and read through the Genesis chapters of his life, past the garden account. Hopefully you'll hang on to the thread throughout, to the book of Revelation, to know what it means for the people of today to have faith that can survive. Because of the cross.

So, I hope, dear friend, if you ever have an opportunity to drop by and eavesdrop on a neighborhood VBS, you'll hear that Bible stories are never just for kids. It may be the only Bible you have at the time.

"Behold, I stand at the door and knock. If anyone hears My voice and opens the door, I will come in to him and dine with him, and he with Me."
Revelation 3:20

pause in the middle

Who was a "Mrs. Landis" to you in your faith journey? What would you say to him or her today if you could?

7
those i met along the way

> *God gives His gifts where He finds the vessel*
> *empty enough to receive them.*
> C. S. LEWIS, *THE QUOTABLE LEWIS*

Early in my faith, the Bible seemed as disjointed as my life. *In the beginning* seemed a good start, but once Leviticus and Numbers came into play, it was over. Instead, I thought a better idea might be to read books written by people who read the Bible. Seemed easier. Not my suggestion for you, but it worked for me.

Remember I was in this thing by myself—party of one. I had no one to disciple me and the *Christianity for Dummies* book wasn't written yet. I was sort of a first-gen Christian in my family. There was no help looking back to any of my begats, except my great-grandfather, John Henry Carter. He was a devout but rigid gentleman who wrote beautiful handwritten letters. Each letter he sent looked like artwork, created with a fountain pen and old-century cursive.

And they went something like this:

Dearest Child, please look into the gospel of John for direction. And I beg you to turn away from the devil's radio, dancing and make up.

So, I skipped the first suggestion, and the rest of it since I was probably putting on mascara and dancing while listening to the radio. However, this dear old soul may have been the only one connected by DNA who was praying for me. And one day many years later, I read the Gospel of John and it changed my life.

I met Jesus in John.

Jesus, the beautifully compassionate nonconformist. It was there that He led me on a journey through the pages that would infuse a strong faith. His message and miracles throughout the Gospel had me see up close how He cared for beggars and healed the blind, loved the lepers and prostitutes. He was drawn to the broken. As I began studying the Scriptures, I saw myself in the many who needed Jesus to reach out and rescue them. And that's all of us.

He grabbed me by the heart and introduced me to a few who He had met and mended along the way.

The Woman at the Well

One lady in particular has left a sacred impression throughout my Christian life. She's simply known as the woman at the well, someone I could easily relate to because she was an empty woman filled with shame who met Jesus and was radically transformed.

And that is so my story.

Her story can be found in John 4:6–19. Most of us know her, but all of us have been her. She is unnamed because I believe she has my name and she has your name. Male and female alike can relate, because we were all once broken and in need of a Savior to fill our emptiness with Living Water.

When we picture this ancient girl, we may get a stained-glass snapshot in our mind of a woman sitting alongside Jacob's Well dressed in first-century desert attire. Maybe you see her resting on her water jar, totally spent from coming in the heat of the day to avoid the gossip. The Samaritan woman is definitely one who has been judged and categorized by assumption.

She's not ancient, she's current. Rejection and shame don't have an expiration date. Women through the ages clothed in garments woven with broken love and despair are still wearing the same label. There are countless women who feel they are defined by the worst thing they've ever done—or that has been done to them. And they're sitting in a nearby pew.

Her story can be found in only one Gospel. We can read between the lines as we travel with Jesus from Judea to Galilee, as most Jews went out of their way to avoid Samaria because the people were considered impure half-breeds. But Jesus went out of His way to go through this place because He was on a God-mission to change one woman's life.

He does the same for you and for me.

It wasn't a chance meeting, because no encounter with Jesus is ever accidental. He didn't pick a random well. Jesus knew right where to find her. He knew she'd come and He knew she'd argue. And He waited for her.

He told her everything she had ever done, but wasn't there to uncover her sin. He knew she filled her well with men, but didn't condemn her. She needed only one Man in this holy moment to change her life forever as she stood emotionally naked before Him.

The tissue-thin pages of the Bible hold the weight of the Gospel dialogue revealed between God and a loathed woman who didn't recognize Him when she came face-to-holy-face. The rejected woman who was considered inferior because of her gender, ethnicity, and multiple relationships engaged in the longest conversation recorded that Jesus had with anyone. She was a woman, a foreigner, and a heretic, and He sought her out to sit down and talk with her.

Jesus makes the most out of one-liners: *"If you knew* the gift of God, and who it is who is saying to you, 'Give me a drink,' you would have asked Him, and He would have given you living water" (v. 11 NASB). The Savior was there to heal her heart, not to count up all the husbands she had and add the guy she was living with. He was there to make a difference in her life that would come to make a difference in the lives of others.

He was there to make her the first evangelist.

So, she ran and told the townspeople, "Come and see!" That's it. No complicated theology or dry, stuffy formula. Just, "Come and see the One who changed my life." It's enough to make a girl drop her water jar and run and tell everyone, don't you think?

This unnamed girl unexpectedly found out who she was and who He was at an old dusty well thousands of years ago, thousands of miles from us. I unexpectedly found out the same amazing truth in the middle of an old dusty pew circa 1975, in Bensalem. And those three words, "If you knew," still echo mercy.

The Son of God will go out of His way in any century or geography to rescue the desperate. He continues to offer Living Water—not just a cup from a stale cistern but a never-ending drink of God. It's just the kind of Savior He is.

We have much in common with our ancient sister. Her story and ours tell a beautiful truth. Jesus intentionally pursues us in our thirst, and He is the only One who can satisfy it.

Jesus intentionally pursues us in our thirst, and He is the only One who can satisfy it.

Dear friend, where is your well? Tell of the sacred encounter when Jesus told you who He was and who you are, and change a life with the power of testimony.

The Woman with the Issue of Blood
Women know what it is to bleed.

Think of a time when you despaired enough to lose hope because nothing seemed like it could change the situation. If you have ever been in that desperate place and thought that it defined you, sit down with this dear lady who is known as the woman with the issue. One of the most unique and healing stories in Scripture is the one of this woman who hemorrhaged.

From the beginning, I was drawn to stories of healing when I became a believer—and it didn't take long to find out why. It seemed the backdrop of my life has been a series of extreme medical issues in our family. So, from the moment I met her, she spoke into my space. This lady made known to me how Jesus heals in response to extreme faith.

She's unnamed, like the woman at the well, but still

important enough for three out of four Gospel writers to tell her story. It's amazing how such a powerful story can be told within three verses in Matthew (9:20–22), six verses in Luke (8:43–48), and the longest version—ten verses in Mark (5:25–34).

This desperate woman was afflicted with a condition that controlled her life for twelve years because no one could change her situation. She spent the little money she had on physicians, but they found no cure for what must have been uterine bleeding.

Adding to the despair, she was considered an unclean outcast. You can read the Jewish law regarding this in Leviticus 15:19–30. She was forbidden to touch anyone, and no one could touch her. Can you imagine a dozen years in isolation? We have a more up-to-date-picture of what that looked like during COVID, with the way people were treated like lepers.

Somehow, she heard about the healing Rabbi and believed that one touch could change the course of her life. Desperation fueled her tenacity to be bold enough to go into the crowd and reach out to Him. If you read Mark's account in chapter 5, the surrounding context tells us a lot was going on. Jesus had just returned from healing a demon-possessed man, and before His sandals hit the shoreline, an important official named Jairus fell at the feet of Jesus to plead with Him to come to his home and heal his only daughter, who was dying. She was only twelve years old—alive as long as the woman seeking out Jesus had been suffering.

Trembling with boldness, the woman approached Jesus from behind, believing if she could get close enough to touch the hem of His garment, she would be healed. She didn't try to get up close and personal to look into His eyes or tap Him on a holy shoulder to get His attention. In her shameful state, her wild faith called her to action to crawl in the dust and no longer remain at the back of the crowd with her clothes stained.

We don't have to walk in her bloody tracks to realize that we share the same path. I hope you see her as a woman who is not much different from any of us, because we have all struggled with something longer than we thought we could.

But she had hemline faith.

With her touch to the fringed edge, Jesus knew something flowed from His body that immediately ceased the flow from hers. And He noticed her. *Her.* The loathed and ostracized was seen. He identified her as "Daughter," and said, "Your faith has made you well."

In so many ways in my small faith, I could relate to this daughter. I could place my distraught self in her quivering shadow because there was the similarity of *twelve* that spoke into those deep cuts in my life where we all bleed red. I knew her centuries-old heart *today* from the bleeding that wouldn't stop in a twelve-year painful marriage or within the plea of a parent begging for a twelve-year-old to survive kidney failure.

As a new believer with little faith, I needed this story, which invited my hand to touch the mystery. Not of power from a hem but of an all-knowing Healer. And all these decades later, I still need this story.

Even now.

The lady who spoke the confession over her life of "If only I may touch His clothes, I shall be made well" teaches us we can do the same to witness His power to flow through our suffering. She was persistent, but came fearful and did it afraid. A radical lady who helps shape our faith is not easy to forget, so I won't.

Her faith made her *not* just cured, *not* just healed, but whole. Allow her faith to challenge you. If your need is desperate, your faith will cause you to push through the crowd of your circumstances. The same power that flowed through the hem of Jesus on that ancient day can be ours today—and we need only to reach out. There's nothing more powerful than a story of a changed woman through the healing touch of God.

The same power that flowed through the hem of Jesus on that ancient day can be ours today— and we need only to reach out.

May we be that woman.

And Others Still

If it wasn't for the Gospel of John in the early days of my search, I would have never visited these holy girls who helped shape my story. Jesus used the Samaritan woman to help me to see my true reflection in the depth of the well. And He knew my chin was scuffing the dust in hopes that I could reach out to a hem that could change the course of my broken life. He knew who we needed to visit first.

So, when I get to heaven, Great-Grandfather John Henry might be the guy I look up first. I believe he was the only one on the begat-family-tree praying for me, and I want him to know that many years after he passed, I finally read the life-changing Gospel that led me on a wonderful journey with Jesus. He never knew because he died when I was thirteen years old. But his prayers never died. Our prayers live on in the ones we've prayed for. Please, pray fervently and be assured of the faith legacy imprint you leave for your children, grands, and greats.

There are sixty-six books in the Bible, and if you honestly seek, you'll find yourself written between the lines on each page. My biblical mentors have changed during different seasons of life, but these two ladies had a dramatic impact on my ability to see who I was in the compassionate eyes of my Savior. We may think of the Bible as a vintage handbook totally outdated and unable to give advice for the complex world we live in today, but I find that no one can help me through present-day problems like the mentors of yesteryear.

When I look back even further, to the Old Testament, those early-century gals can tell a twenty-first century *us* a few things about wild faith. I think of the clever and courageous mom of Moses, Jochebed. Her story is in Exodus 2:1–10 (or you can see her every year in *The Ten Commandments* on television). Her Hollywood name is pronounced "YOASH-a-bell" (which makes as little sense as the pronunciation of Nebuchadnezzar). This faithful, sacrificing mother showed me how to surrender what I treasured most and trust God's will in the middle of a crocodile-infested Nile. Just let go of the basket.

Gentle Hannah taught me how to hope and pray through impossibilities. Her empty womb was miraculously filled with a prophet (1 Samuel 1–2). Naomi and other widows in the Bible came alongside to encourage me through the loss of my husband and soulmate. And although not a woman, the one who got me through the night was the shepherd-king David, pouring out songs of comfort in the Psalms while teaching me to purge on journal pages.

Those we meet along the way, featured in a holy book, are the extraordinary ordinary. Those we meet along the everyday path that winds through life are just as extraordinary because in some way they have been used to shape our faith.

And then we live and follow and shape others' faith.

Jesus said to _____, "I who speak to you am He. Your faith has made you whole. Go in peace." (from Mark 5:34; John 4:26)

pause in the middle

Who has shaped your faith, and whose faith do you want to shape?

8
what's your name—who's your daddy?

Forgive me for being so ordinary while claiming to know so extraordinary a God.

JIM ELLIOT

We've all heard the saying "It's all in who you know." And when it comes to God, that's definitely true. Because knowing God means everything. *Everything.*

Knowing God is the difference between victory and defeat, between rest and turmoil, between going to bed anxious and waking up with hope, and definitely between life and death. If you agree, then you have the hope and assurance of heaven. But there will be moments when we second-guess it all.

So, I have asked myself, *Do I really know Him and know that He really knows me—and when did I know that I knew?*

I think we can all say we know God because, after all, He's famous. But knowing is not *knowing*. We have become so over-familiar with God that we don't know the holy HIM. A good Bible study girl with a head full of sermons and conferences can become just a container for information with little revelation or intimacy. So, familiarity can be the enemy of our faith.

Recently, I was chatting with someone who identified as an atheist and summed it up as ego and arrogance to presume that anyone could know God. His stance was that we don't really know our family or friends in the way that we think we do, so how could we possibly know a God? Makes sense if you don't look deeper.

My husband and I were married for nearly forty years. We knew how the other one thought, and most times could finish each other's sentences, but there is a limit to what we can know about another in the soul-deep recess.

The mysterious difference in the way we can *know that we know* God and experience intimacy with heaven is only because of the Holy Spirit. When we come to Christ, He lives *within* us. It's internal. Can't get closer than internal. In His extravagant mercy, He seeks us out to make Himself known, even if we refuse to acknowledge Him (see Romans 1:20).

Back in the younger-self day, I prayed to a God I didn't know. Something drew me to a place I didn't understand, but a loving Father understood that I didn't understand. It is no small thing for us to have the right to address a holy God as a loving Father. The Bible is clear that He is a good Father and tells us we have the right to call Him *Abba*, an ancient Aramaic term for "daddy." I wanted to understand that. I wanted to know Him by name.

God, what's Your name?

It is no small thing for us to have the right to address a holy God as a loving Father.

Knowing God's names can radically change the way we relate to Him. I used to think it was watering down His majesty when I heard Him referred to as a Daddy. But when we can see God as our Abba Papa, we will embrace our identity as daughter and see the Bible as a story our Father reads to us. Once I experienced salvation, I found out quickly that there is a greater depth of knowing God than just confessing faith. It wasn't just about knowing Him, but how to *keep* knowing Him.

When we're introduced to someone, one of the first things we ask is their name; otherwise they may simply remain an acquaintance. Names are of value—they tell who we are even if we have the same one as the person sitting right next to us (obviously, that never happened to me). And don't you hate when you forget someone's name? I don't want to forget God's name. To forget His name is to forget His character.

Someone who taught me the importance of God's names and has been instrumental in shaping my faith is well-known Bible teacher Kay Arthur, co-founder of Precept International Ministries. From the time I was a new believer and up to present day, Kay has been a strong influence in my life through her teaching and Bible studies. This lady has dedicated her life to knowing Jesus and making Him known. Through her I met God by name and discovered the powerful meaning revealed in each Hebrew name that holds the answer to every situation in life.

One of the first life-changing books I read was *Lord, I Want to Know You*, a topical study written by Kay in the early 1980s. It was written in a way to meet the reader where they are. At the time I felt unsafe, afraid of God's will because of all that had taken place in my life.

I opened the book and turned to the name *El Elyon*, the

God Most High. The name means "sovereign," which means nothing happens without Him knowing about it and giving permission for it to touch our lives.

Hmmm. I had to ponder that one at the time. I wanted to believe He knew about my little boy who was suffering at the hands of doctors and that he would need miracles to bring him through multiple transplants over the years. I needed to believe that He knew about all that was coming our way and how it would teach me to trust in the midst of tragedy. So that it wasn't just in vain.

This holy name, *El Elyon*, is the one that brought me through when doctors stood over three dying sons and my comatose husband and said there was nothing more they knew to do. This is the name I called upon—His sovereignty. And He heard me call His name.

Each hallowed Hebrew name of God demonstrates the powerful meaning that holds the answer to every circumstance in life. So, allow me to reintroduce Him.

Dear you, this is your creator and shepherd; your provider and healer; your banner who covers, watches over, and sanctifies; your peace and righteousness; and the One who will remain present and fight for you—and who is pleased to meet you.

- *Elohim*, the Creator God, is the first one we're introduced to in the pages of Scripture (Genesis 1).
- *El Elyon* is the sovereign controller of the universe. He sustains His people through every trial on planet earth and yet is the ruler of heaven (Genesis 14).
- *El Roi* is the God who sees, watches over His

creation with a holy eye, and knows us by name (Genesis 16).
- *El Shaddai* reveals His bounty as the nourisher and the almighty (Genesis 17).
- *Adonai* is our master and owner of it all (Genesis 15).
- *Jehovah Jireh* is our provision in want and in plenty (Genesis 22).
- *Jehovah Rapha* is our healer, the only One who can cure a sin sick world (Exodus 15).
- *Jehovah Nissi* is our banner, the One who fights our battles (Exodus 17).
- *Jehovah Shalom* is the God of our peace told in the story of Gideon (Judges).
- *Jehovah Sabaoth* is the Lord of Hosts, the God of angel armies in time of defeat (1 Samuel 1).
- *Jehovah Raah* is our Shepherd who directs our path and sometimes carries us (Ezekiel 34).
- *Jehovah Shammah* is "the Lord is there." His personal presence surrounds us (Ezekiel 48).

Did you know God's name is woven throughout the Twenty-third Psalm to unveil His character in greater depth? Take a look:

> The LORD is my shepherd; (Jehovah **Raah,**
>   our guide; v. 1)
> I shall not want. (Jehovah **Jireh,** our
>   provider; v. 2)
> He makes me to lie down in green pastures;
> He leads me beside the still waters. (Jehovah
>   **Shalom,** our peace; v. 2)

He restores my soul; (Jehovah **Rapha**, our
  healer; v. 3)
He leads me in paths of righteousness
For His name's sake. (Jehovah **Tsidkenu**, our
  righteousness; v. 3)
Yea, though I walk through the valley of the
  shadow of death, I will fear no evil;
for you are with me, your rod and staff they
  comfort me. (Jehovah **Shammah,** the
  Lord is present; v. 4)
You prepare a table before me in the presence
  of my enemies; (Jehovah **Nissi**, our
  banner; v. 5)
You anoint my head with oil;
My cup runs over. (Jehovah **M'Kaddesh,** our
  sanctification; v. 5).
Surely goodness and mercy shall follow me
All the days of my life;
And I will dwell in the house of the LORD
Forever! (v. 6)

Yes, we've all heard the saying "It's all in who you know." And it is.

The Father longs to have _____ know Him better so that she can trust in the name of the Lord and rely on Him. (from Isaiah 30:18)

verna bowman

pause in the middle

What name(s) of God have you leaned on most? Why?

pause in the middle

9
seen and known

> *You are looked at by God as much as if throughout space there were no other creatures but yourself.*
> CHARLES SPURGEON

You are seen and you are known. *Really.* We come across people every day who are desperately hurting and lonely and questioning whether anyone can see them in a crowd of needs—especially God. Today I went to Thursday morning Bible study with over fifty Jesus-lovin' women. And of course, there were over fifty-ish prayer concerns in that room. Later, I listened to the six o'clock news and realized once again how seven billion people who occupy this planet have seven billion needs.

And yet, I know what I know. There is none like God who has created a universe and oversees mere things like gravity and quantums, so I'm convinced the omniscient God knows me, the one among billions. And you. There were too many times in my life when I knew He *had to be* or I wouldn't be writing to tell about it.

The eyes of the LORD run to and fro throughout the whole earth, to show Himself strong on behalf of those whose heart is loyal to Him. (2 Chronicles 16:9)

If we truly believed this verse, we would live differently, pray differently, and see ourselves as God sees us. For some, it can be more of a curse than a blessing to know God has His eye on us. Instead of thinking God is watching over us because He adores us, we imagine Him tracking our moves to catch us in the act. This little piece of theology makes a huge difference in how we perceive God and how we think He perceives us.

When hard things touch our lives, one of the last things we want to hear is "God sees this and has a plan." How can we make it real, instead of sounding like another empty platitude that gets in the way of our reality? Especially for the homeless, the trafficked, the war-zone orphan. Do they feel seen and known?

If you're experiencing a season when you're asking, "Where is God?" and "Does He know me even a little bit?" I encourage you to read Psalm 139. But before you do, I want to share a short story of when *I knew what I didn't know.*

One of my close childhood friends was Mary. Mary Magdalene was her exact beautiful name. I grew up in a Catholic neighborhood during the Mary era, so I had a Mary Katherine two streets over, a Mary Theresa down the hill, and a Mary Margaret next door. I'm sure a Mary Elizabeth was nearby.

My friend Mary had a devout Hungarian-Catholic mother. This dear lady walked to the neighborhood parish a few miles away a few times a week, for as long as I can remember. And when she didn't walk, she rode her daughter's bicycle. She was dedicated. And I didn't get it. Nobody in my house even went to church on Christmas, so I wasn't sure what the draw was.

When I was in sixth grade, one of our classmates, Bobby, was hit by a car while riding his bike after school. Later that day as I was walking past his house, I could hear his mother crying—the kind of guttural cry that tells a tragic story. I ran home to ask my mom what could be wrong, and she quietly explained that Bobby was in critical condition and not expected to live. That night and the next and the next, I couldn't get the sound of his mother's pain out of my heart.

I felt helpless as a young girl, but thought if I could get to the church where Mary's mother would go and asked her God to allow my friend to live, his mother wouldn't be so heartbroken. For the next three weeks, I rode my bike across forbidden Brownsville Road (where the accident occurred) up to the BVM Assumption every day.

I was afraid to walk through the heavy doors, not knowing what was on the other side. But in I went. It was silent and sacred inside. It smelled like God lived there. And it was mysteriously peaceful, filled with the fragrance of a loving Father who bowed low to meet a child who was seen and known by Him, crying out for a grieving mother and a dying boy. And Bobby lived.

And soon, I rode my bike home and left God in the dust.

Ten years later, another dear friend I grew up with was diagnosed with stage four cancer and not expected to live. I remember the call from her heartbroken mother. By then I was twenty-two years old, married with two children, and didn't know the Lord any better than I did when I was twelve. But for some reason, I drove miles back to that church to ask the God of Mary's mother to once again allow another friend to live. And He did. She lived for fifty more years.

And sadly, I drove back home and left God in the dust.

It was hard to understand then—and sometimes hard to understand even now. I was as far away from God as anyone could be, but in the middle of a rebellious life I was seen and I was known. As near as my breath, it was as if I was called to be an intercessor for broken women before I knew Jesus. *Even then.*

> **I was as far away from God as anyone could be, but in the middle of a rebellious life I was seen and I was known.**

I share this story because it's not simply mine. It's also yours. He answered prayers then and He answers still. I was twelve a long time ago, but when I go back home nearly twenty-five miles away, I pull up to the little empty church and open the heavy doors to the sacred place that smells like God lives there. I sit down in the same time-worn pew as a reminder of how real and personal my Father has been to me over the years as I've been the hurting mom crying out for my own dying sons.

I'm grateful to this devout neighborhood lady who indirectly introduced a rebel kid to the God of her heart. Her daily trek inspired me to search for something I hoped was there. She never knew the mark she left on my life and has long gone to heaven. It doesn't matter that her faith was found in beads and statues, incense and candles. What matters is that I witnessed devotion in action that left tracks on my heart to this day, so thank you, Mary Magdalene's mom.

Later, when I began to walk with Jesus, the Bible reassured me that we are seen by our Father. Psalm 139 tells us that long before the sperm met the egg, we were known. And the very first book of the Bible tells how God sees and knows us.

Within the story of Abram and Sarai (later renamed Abraham and Sarah) is the story of an Egyptian servant named Hagar. She was a kicked-to-the-ditch lady I could personally relate to when she was abandoned and had to fend for herself in the wilderness. In Genesis 16, the old couple who were waiting for the promised son were still waiting, so Sarai suggested her maid have a baby. Abram consented, and Hagar had no choice. The Lord knew the nation He would birth within her womb, and she had a son, Ishmael, called a wild donkey of a man (Genesis 16:12).

And wouldn't you know, the promised son Isaac came after Abram and Sarai took matters into their own hands. Rivalry. Two girls never like sharing a man, no matter how far back you look. So, Hagar had to hit the road (actually for a second time), this time with her child. But God saw her and rescued her from the bitter unfairness. And this made her see Him. She encountered Him so intimately that she was the only person in the entire Bible who gives God a name. She called Him *El Roi*, the God who sees.

> She gave this name to the LORD who spoke to her: "You are the God who sees me," for she said, "I have now seen the One who sees me." (Genesis 16:13 NIV)

There are so many stories in the Bible that we can relate to. Trauma can uncover itself quickly with just a look back. And when I do, I remember how excited I was to be pregnant after three miscarriages after my first son. My older children were ten and eight years old. It was a high-risk pregnancy that I had to fight to keep, but I felt confident I would go full term and that the Lord had a special purpose for this child at this time in my life. And He did.

I came to Jesus during this pregnancy in 1975. This was when life took a huge turn, which is why I went into some detail a few stories back.

To describe this as a difficult pregnancy due to the physical concerns would be an understatement compared to the emotional abuse in my marriage. Then finding out that my husband was involved with our best friend's teenage daughter was far worse than the countless affairs with women from the past. I felt alone, rejected, and totally done. But God protected me and my unborn son. And I could say the same as Hagar: "I have seen the One who sees me."

It was only the Lord who could rescue me from the place I had been. I asked myself the question God asked Hagar in the wilderness of her life: "Where have you come from and where are you going?" It's a question that all of us need to answer.

If you have difficulty believing that you are beautifully known, these selected verses from Psalm 139 assure us that the Lord has a biography written of each one of us even before we were born. We can rest in between every line, knowing that we are seen. If you read all twenty-four verses in your Bible, you'll see it can't get more personal than this.

Hurting friend, God sees you in the dialysis clinic, through every chemotherapy appointment, next to a sick child's bed, distraught in the unemployment line, mourning at the edge of a gravesite, and He knows every despairing thing you will ever face. To be seen and known is the difference between going to bed anxious and waking up hopeless, and knowing you don't have to do either.

verna bowman

O Lord, You have searched me and
    known me.
You know my sitting down and my rising up;
You understand my thought afar off.
You comprehend my path and my lying
    down,
And are acquainted with all my ways.
For there is not a word on my tongue,
But behold, O Lord, You know it altogether.
You have hedged me behind and before,
And laid Your hand upon me.
Such knowledge is too wonderful for me;
It is high, I cannot attain it.
Where can I go from Your Spirit?
Or where can I flee from Your presence?
If I ascend into heaven, You are there;
If I make my bed in hell, behold, You are
    there.
If I take the wings of the morning,
And dwell in the uttermost parts of the sea,
Even there Your hand shall lead me,
And Your right hand shall hold me.
If I say, "Surely the darkness shall fall
    on me,"
Even the night shall be light about me;
Indeed, the darkness shall not hide from You,
But the night shines as the day;
The darkness and the light are both
    alike to You.
For You formed my inward parts;
You covered me in my mother's womb.
I will praise You, for I am fearfully and won-
    derfully made;

Marvelous are Your works,
And that my soul knows very well.
My frame was not hidden from You,
When I was made in secret,
And skillfully wrought in the lowest parts of
    the earth.
Your eyes saw my substance, being yet
    unformed.
And in Your book they all were written,
The days fashioned for me,
When as yet there were none of them.
(Psalm 139:1–16)

> *The Lord watches over _____.*
> *The Lord is your shade at your right hand; the sun*
> *will not harm you by day nor the moon by night.*
> *The Lord will keep _____ from harm*
> *and watch over your life.*
> *(from Psalm 121:5–6)*

pause in the middle

So, friend, where have you come from and where are you going?

10
on the days i can believe

Faith isn't acting like circumstances don't exist.
It's acting like they don't rule over your existence.
UNKNOWN

Belief is a big deal to God. It's not enough just to believe. We need to believe that He is trustworthy.

Wild trust is essential for the times we're living in right now. There are some days that are enough to make one shudder. But looking back, way back into the archives of history, wild trust is an absolute understatement.

God's people were called to major tasks. Imagine building an ark when it wasn't even drizzling. Or taking one step closer to Moriah with an armload of kindling to sacrifice an only and long-awaited son. Or walking around Jericho for seven days and expecting walls to fall. Or worse, getting thrown into a den of lions and hoping they just ate. These things happened to those who had to choose to believe on the hard days. On the hardest days.

Some argue that God no longer does miracles today, but He didn't stop being incredible at the end of the Bible.

Their stories weren't breathed onto Bible pages for debate or entertainment, but to bring us to a faith that passes all understanding. *Miraculous* faith. Some argue that God no longer does miracles today, but He didn't stop being incredible at the end of the Bible. The Greek meaning of the word *miracle* literally means "wonder at, be amazed at." Maybe you've seen a few *unexplainables* in your time, when you've stood in awe and wondered over. I certainly have, because of or despite the limitations of humans. If I didn't believe miracles are for today, I would have no hope.

Because I need one now.

When we look back to the beginning and try to process the crazy faith it took for Moses to face a raging sea, believing it would come apart in the nick of time, or for Abraham and Sarah to wait for nearly a century before sending out birth announcements, we have to ask ourselves why it's so hard for us who live in what appears to be a technology-cakewalk kind of life to get through the day without a drink, pill, or therapist.

No shred of imagination can connect me to the dramatic events that God's people experienced back then, but some of our own dark and dangerous stories can seem just as terrifying. And that's because life has never been a cakewalk. Then or now.

But despite the amazing faith and courage, the Bible also tells us that these stories weren't without doubts and struggles. As believers living in any age, all of us have experienced a Red Sea moment—an impossible situation when only God can miraculously part the waves of circumstances that are trying to bury our scared soul—at one time or another. And I'll testify of the seas we've crossed.

I like to believe that if I'm standing on the edge of the deep, I can trust an almighty hand to rescue me before I go under. Until I get too close to the edge, that is. The honesty of my faith (and maybe yours) can be found at the edge. When the deep threatens to swallow, we struggle with flexible faith that is willing to bend. In times like these, and I had one just yesterday, I have to get close enough to lay down in His shadow, and I plead loud and long to feel brave again.

My relationship with God has been complicated, never complacent. The times I had to choose like Job to not turn away have been many but have caused me to cling all the more. Sometimes life is too much to bear when we bear another's burden and it becomes ours. When the heartbreak of another's story is written into ours, it makes it more difficult to survive our own.

I have prayed for over half my life (literally) for one deep concern. Although I have a beautiful knowledge of who my Father is, I realize that I'm praying to a God who made Abraham wait, who made the Israelites walk in a desert for too long, and who showed up in strange ways to declare His will in His way, His time. Complicated.

Life is hard but God is good, and don't confuse the two.

As I'm writing this, there are hard things going on in my life, some too hard to put to words. Through my son's transplant journey—our family's transplant journey, actually—I've had the "'scuse me while I kiss the sky" moments when God feels so close. But then there are the "why are you taking us on this runaway train wreck" moments when I don't know if I can keep holding on. So, no words right now.

As I journal the words I can't write here, I know I'm not the only one who feels they've been given more than they can handle. I think of the string of words that gets so easily tangled—"God won't give you more than you can handle"—which are not true and not in the Bible. Obviously, if we had no trouble handling ugly life, we wouldn't need Jesus.

We can never know what is up His sovereign sleeve, so we must trust. Trust isn't something we can just manufacture. Since I'm fresh out of new ideas, I fall back on the ones I know have worked for me. One way to trust God is to stop trusting yourself. The other is to remember. There is no way I can trust in this place called *here*, between the past and the next, if I don't remember how God has never left me down.

And I have a life verse I cling to like an anchor . . .

> I would have despaired UNLESS I had believed that I would see the goodness of the Lord in the land of the living. Wait for the Lord; be strong and let your heart take courage. (Psalm 27:13 NASB1995)

What these God-breathed words mean to me, if not for the confidence that God comes through to bring victory in this life here on earth and not just in heaven, I would give up. So, I believe to see.

I think it must have meant the same to David when he wrote this psalm of fearless trust for the times I'm sure he was shaking in his sandals. All fourteen verses of Psalm 27 will sit on the steps of your soul to prove you can remain steadfast because He is steadfast. Only reason.

Think of your *right now impossible* that only a Deliverer can bring you through. And if He chooses not to, do you have the faith to believe He is still good? I want to be her who did, who does, who will.

I want to be her . . . Mary of Bethany who lets the world pass by at His feet.

I want to be her . . . Mary of Bethlehem who says may it be no matter the uncertain journey.

I want to be her . . . the hemorrhaging woman who believes enough to reach for a holy hem.

I want to be her . . . the woman who overflows from one meeting at the well.

I *want* to be, but I'm not. And when faith fails, I remember I'm just *her* who is His.

Blessed is _____ who believed, for there will be a fulfillment of those things which were told her from the Lord. (from Luke 1:45)

pause in the middle

Is there a concern of your heart that you have trouble believing God will answer?

11
what if one line could tell your story?

"Lord I believe; help my unbelief."
MARK 9:24

If you tuned in to a June 2021 episode of *America's Got Talent*, you may have been as moved as millions of others by the singer known as Nightbirde. She alone brought the usually cold Simon Cowell to tears when she performed her original song "It's Okay."

The song tells of the last year of her battle with cancer, which she fought hard through three times before turning thirty years old. It's hard to imagine that she faced this difficult time while also going through a divorce. I'm sure she felt defeated and alone.

But she knew God on the days she couldn't believe.

I hold onto her compassionate echo, "You are so much more than the bad things that happened to you."[1] I play the phrase over and over on the days I can't believe it. We can get paralyzed with self-pity when things appear hopeless.

We know and believe until we take a pen to our journal and write out boldly "Why?" a thousand times.

Why cancer and disease, why war and floods, why trafficking and murder, why the fall that caused it all? And we can't stop it. We can't understand it. So we either trust or worry. To worry is to have a conversation with yourself about something you can't do anything about.

To worry is to have a conversation with yourself about something you can't do anything about.

In Matthew 6, Jesus tells us to take no thought to worry about the things of this life. He gave us the heads-up that we would have trouble in this world, but we don't have to let the cares hold us captive. We can dwell on the character and faithfulness of God rather than what might happen. And even if the unthinkable happens, we dwell on Him anyway. Some say, "That might be easy for you but not for me." Well, no, it's not easy for any of us. But it is doable if we train ourselves to think differently, even in the middle of the night when we chase sleep but our mind keeps winning the race.

Sadly, Nightbirde lost her fight with cancer, but her beauty and bravery lives on in a simple one-liner: "You can't wait until life isn't hard anymore before you decide to be happy."[2]

The secret to surviving the middle on the days we *can* believe is told in fourteen words. Thank you, Jane Marczewski, for leaving a legacy of your beautiful faith on the days you could believe.

In the Gospel of Luke, we're reminded nothing is impossible with God. If there were no other verse in the Bible but this one, it would be enough for me to walk through the trials I have faced. I hope it's enough for you when you're not certain if you can take another step forward.

For I am persuaded that neither death nor life, nor angels nor principalities nor powers, nor things present nor things to come, nor height nor depth, nor any other created thing, shall be able to separate _____ from the love of God which is in Christ Jesus our Lord.
(from Romans 8:38–39)

even now

pause in the middle

What one line can tell your story?

12
the middle of the stairwell

*Faith is taking the first step even
when you don't see the whole staircase.*
MARTIN LUTHER KING JR.

It was one of those overwhelming days. I drove home not knowing how I got there. I walked into a house, not sure if it was mine. The key fit into a door I wish I didn't have to go through. No one was on the other side after tragedy had taken my family in three different directions.

I wasn't sure if I pulled into my own driveway after coming home from the inner-city hospital where my youngest son was rejecting a third kidney transplant. Or maybe it was from the suburban hospital where my husband was rehabilitating after suffering multiple strokes. Then again, it could have been from the trauma center located in between where another son was fighting for his life after a near-fatal car accident.

I only knew I had reached the end—wherever it was. My wit's end—whatever it is.

I finally reached the place where it had been too much for too long. Far too many waiting rooms, negative reports, hospital sounds and smells, too many distressed people. I found myself just going through the motions on the same familiar path I had for so many years, but now all of it converged into a moment. I was tired of being faithful and believing for better.

I walked into the dark foyer of my home and threw my keys and purse wherever they dropped. And I did the same. Dropped. In the middle of the stairwell. On my knees, I cried out to more than the ceiling with the last prayer I had left: "Father, put Your hand up and say no more!"

I thought this, right here, must be what it's like when the story ends and there are no other chapters. *Just this one. This constant one.*

I honestly didn't know who to grieve more. My husband, my sons, or myself.

I was too exhausted to go up the stairs, there was no one there. I was too weary to go down the stairs, there was no one there. I simply remained in the middle—in the frightening and lonely middle. But for some reason I felt safe there, away from where I had been all day and all night.

This trifold trauma in our family took place many years ago, yet it doesn't take much to remind me of what I felt in the middle of the stairwell. And it was far from my mind on a particular day while away with a few dear friends for a weekend, though. We rented an Airbnb in a small New Jersey shore town, hoping it would stir some inspiration into the current writing projects we were working on. We were having a great time sharing ideas with lots of laughter, when somehow the direction shifted into a more serious conversation about surviving challenging times. Of course, we all had examples.

Close friends know many of our stories. Or they think they do. Carolyn makes sure she finds the one we aren't ready to share. She asks questions that can't be answered on the spot. She's gifted that way. She leaned over the table and asked me in the face, "So much has happened in your life that takes a strong faith. There must have been a time when that faith wavered, right?"

I made the mistake of answering her loaded question right away. "Of course. Many times."

Carolyn peered over her glasses, which always makes her appear instantly wiser, and met my gaze. "I don't want many. I want *one*." She's pretty tricky.

Wow, I had so many to choose from. I doubt whether I would have thought back to this triple-slam that hit all the same time without her holy prodding.

"Can you write about it?" she asked.

I went into the bedroom by myself to do that, knowing there was no use coming back from the other room to face her with an empty journal. So, twenty minutes later I brought her the story of *just one*: "In the Middle of the Stairwell."

By the way, thank you, Carolyn. It's amazing what can happen when we uncover something that needs to be processed rather than just accepted. I understood that an explosive time involving three family members who were in critical condition all at the same time needed to be revisited in order to give myself permission to feel rather than compartmentalize into the dark backdrop.

I felt lost in everyone's story that covered up my own. When it comes to praying for healing, our theology can get twisted. Carolyn's mini therapy session made me realize it was okay to fold and feel fainthearted. It was okay to question and become so numb that I couldn't read my Bible or pray. *It was okay.*

Dear friend, it's in the *middle of the stairwell* that we find the sanctuary within the madness when we invite Jesus to come and sit on the steps of our soul to remind us of the times He has rescued us in the past. Even when it feels like all hope is lost, hope will always find you if your soul remembers. Perseverance is taking one more step, even if it's only one.

Perseverance is taking one more step, even if it's only one.

Now, back to my stairwell.

Once again, with the Savior's help, I did get back up to take another step during one of the hardest seasons for our family. You may be facing a time right now where you feel like you're knocking at a door without anyone home. I pray you will hang in. If you're there, you need more than just a good Bible study girl to share another story, so instead I share my heart.

And a story—a Gospel story about a persistent widow who persevered instead of throwing in the towel. She was alone and helpless and had a deep plea that went unanswered. It would have been easy to give up. Jesus used her story as a parable to illustrate to His disciples how they should pray and never give up because effective prayer requires tenacity and faithfulness.

I understood her. I was her. A widow with a plea. And known to be tenacious. Jesus tells her story this way . . .

"There was a judge in a certain city," he said, "who neither feared God nor cared about people. A widow of that city came to him repeatedly, saying, 'Give me justice in this dispute with my enemy.' The judge ignored her for a while, but finally he said to himself, 'I don't fear God or care about people, but this woman is driving me crazy. I'm going to see that she gets justice, because she is wearing me out with her constant requests!'" Then the Lord said, "Learn a lesson from this unjust judge. Even he rendered a just decision in the end. So don't you think God will surely give justice to his chosen people who cry out to him day and night? Will he keep putting them off? I tell you, he will grant justice to them quickly! But when the Son of Man returns, how many will he find on the earth who have faith?" (Luke 18:1-8 NLT)

The widow persistently went to this unjust judge with the same request. He had no compassion, so he did not represent God. Jesus used this example of an unjust judge because if he would listen to the woman's request and grant justice, how much more will a loving Father?

She could've accepted *it is what it is*, but instead she bothered this guy until she wore him down to *it doesn't have to stay this way*. She believed in her God and she believed in herself. I want to be her—the one who remains steadfast to have courage to believe to see until she hears the last *no*. And believe it won't be.

I first read the persistent widow's story years ago while in an ICU waiting room. It's where I learned what *tenacious* means. I don't know of a lonelier place than a waiting room in the middle of the night. It's like sitting in a train station and the train doesn't come. But sitting in a waiting room in the middle of the day is almost worse, because it's like sitting in a train station after the wreck. Too much of the unknown.

I've heard some Bible teachers and preachers say that once you've asked God for something, it displays lack of faith if you ask again since you ought to believe you have already received it (see Mark 11:24). Yep, it's a tricky mix. But Jesus teaches clearly that we are to continue to pray until we receive the answer. That's not little faith, that's persistent faith.

When we're stuck in the middle and our prayer becomes a weak whisper of, "Lord, how long?," it's then we need to take the next step and the next. It comes with wrestling and resting, giving ourselves no respite from our endeavor in prayer.

Blessed is _____, who perseveres under trial having stood the test and will receive the crown of life that the Lord has promised to those who love Him.
(from James 1:12)

pause in the middle

What circumstances are you facing right now that are tempting you to lose heart or making you feel faint?

13
when seasons change

Change is the scenery along the path, not the end of the road.
UNKNOWN

I love this quote because I'm just a girl peddling hope.
However, there are times when we can't help but feel the end of the road is . . . *here*. When we come to the very edge of nothing ahead.

"There's nothing we can do" is one of the most final things we can hear. Those five words can bring a close to a chapter in life like nothing else—especially when spoken by a doctor. The words can only mean one thing: we need a miracle. It certainly left no room for hope on the day when the stone-faced medical team approached me outside of my husband's hospital room.

I thought I would be ready when I had to hear this, but no. We never are.

Looking down, I felt lower than the floor and responded

in a defeated whisper, "I've heard this before, so I've learned when to fight and when to surrender."

One of them said, "Then this is the time to surrender."

Change is inevitable, but can we ever be ready for the big changes?

I couldn't help but think, *I am so tired of people in scrubs bearing bad news.*

This was a season-changing, life-changing day. It was Valentine's Day. I thought, *No matter how this is ending, I will always remember how it began.*

Jeff, the miracle guy who seemed invincible, was once strong enough to build a house for his family, push a car uphill while the emergency brake was on (I'm still pretty sorry about that), and hold up through years of multiple afflictions. Now he was frail and weak, needing the help of two nurses to get him into a chair next to his hospital bed. The powerful hands that built our home alongside our Bible study friends were now too feeble to hold a photograph.

I was hesitant to go into his room. I didn't have words to take with me. He stared down, teary-eyed and smiling, while holding tightly to the framed memory of the two of us walking strong together in Pittsburgh only months before. Then it dropped and shattered, like broken memories during the many times that life shattered in our nearly four decades together.

Jeff and I were used to dealing with broken, yet this was by far the hardest. I sat on the edge of his bed to carefully relay the decision that had been made by the doctors. It was final.

He understood—dialysis would no longer be needed and the defibrillator implant would be removed so that it wouldn't trick his body into staying alive. Turning off an

ICD doesn't hasten death, but it will prevent a dying patient from receiving shocks while the heart is failing.

But our days are ordained by the One who has the decision in His hands. *I know*.

Jeff listened to what I had to say and reached for my hand. "Japheth knows what to do, then." Jeff had already selected the praise and worship songs that he'd asked our oldest grandson to sing at his memorial celebration. The beautiful image remains in my heart of Japheth sitting by Jeff's hospice bed, singing those handpicked songs of comfort as Jesus ushered him home.

Unlike the beginning of his life growing up in an orphanage, the end of his life was surrounded with those who loved him. His daughter slept by his hospice bedside during his last days. His sons kept vigil one day at a time, reminding him of who he had been to them. His grandchildren gathered around a deathbed and stayed with him until final breath. Our son-in-law and grandson beautifully crafted the casket—a prepared resting place with the inside of the lid etched with a loving message, Scripture verse, or hymn lyric by each of the kids and grandkids.

It was a season like no other, when broken hearts hid in the bleak February winter of soul.

When we lose our person, it's as if the other half that helped us breathe is gone.

even now

Journal entry, February 2016

Jeff's Christmas watch is still on the night table. It's 9:30pm, reminding me that time is going on without him. But how?

Time passes and runs into the next moment before we get there. And so how did we get to the place when time ran out? It never runs out in the heavenlies, so you'll be okay, Jeff.

I think of all he would have missed, we would have missed, if I had agreed to discontinue the life support ten years ago. Most of all, I wouldn't have wanted to miss all the grace.

Jeff was a guy whose body broke down piece by piece, but nothing could break his spirit. Like a death sentence, one letter at a time, yet life was extended by tying miracles together.

His last project was sitting at the dining room table—going through old photos of the kids and grandkids, as though the scrapbooks were opening the gifts that meant the most to him.

There is no stillness like the stillness of half of you leaving while the other half tries to remain. It gives new meaning to be still and know—can we know God's presence when life becomes this still or hope to get through when we don't?

I have laid in His shadow to cling-close. Because I need Him to be that near right now . . .

You alone know, O Lord ~ Ezekiel 37:3

When Jeff left for heaven, the year 2016 was what brought the most change in my life. After all, he was the one who walked the *uphill* path with me from the time I was a single mom with three children. Three children whose lives would not have been the same without him. He was the one who cried with me and rejoiced with me through Geoff's transplant journey. The one who shared my pride when children graduated, married, and gave us the gift of grandchildren. He was brilliant enough to hold high positions, but when life folded, he was humble enough to rake blacktop to provide for his family. He was the guy who no one could ever replace in my life.

But if I'm honest, there were countless times when I felt *stuck* because of the weariness of caregiving through the long years of illness. It was a time of suffering and grieving before the grief. Caregiving is a precious gift that we give of ourselves to another. As Jeff became more infirm and dependent, we had to both go forward in our own way, together. After spending almost half my life with him, I couldn't allow him to face it alone even though I was feeling just as alone. It makes deep meaning of the vow "in sickness and in health, to love and to cherish, till death us do part."

It's hard to see that faraway place while standing young and able at the altar. But *someday* always comes.

I continually had to reframe my perspective to remember the times *before* the picture shattered. Six months before Jeff passed, an organization that grants wishes to critically ill seniors contacted us. We were told how some choose adventurous things like skydiving, some choose visiting a faraway vacation spot where they've never been, but Jeff chose a trip to Pittsburgh. A place across the state, where we had visited several times before. He could have chosen anything or anywhere, but he chose to return to where the trees had grown seventy years taller in a place where his father and grandfather walked. His beautifully simple wish.

Earlier that year, before the Wish of a Lifetime organization trip, we were contacted by *The 700 Club* to have Jeff's miraculous recovery from a coma featured on an episode. It tells a devastatingly beautiful story of how he received his life back after being declared brain dead with only 2 percent brain activity. Our family was told that it was irreversible, and strongly encouraged to discontinue the life support because there was no hope of recovery. I refused and made the decision to wait seven days, knowing what God can do.

Miraculously, Jeff woke up on the seventh morning and lived another fifteen years. After a long and arduous rehabilitation, he was able to return to work and live a fairly normal life. You can tune in to the video of "On the Brink of Death" on the media tab at www.vernabowman.com or on cbn.com with a name search on *The 700 Club*.

More change and loss followed after the great loss of my husband. One month later, I sold my home to relocate closer to my family. Packing up and transporting memories was difficult to do within thirty days. Next, I lost my medical office job of twenty-five years after the physicians retired. Worse, the church I had been part of for nearly forty years was coming apart before it actually fell apart. I didn't want to leave, I didn't want to stay. I felt misplaced and had no idea where I belonged. The lifeline came undone when I was no longer in my marriage, my home, my workplace, or my church. Everything changed, so I had to . . . too.

Adding to the struggle, my daughter was going through a huge change in her personal life. At the same time, my oldest son was battling cancer while going through a custody dispute for his son. All together, it complicated the grieving process further.

Shortly after is when my younger son rejected his kidney at the beginning of the COVID-19 pandemic. A year later, I suffered a widow-maker heart attack and had to have an LED stent in the artery. This was another unexplained event—no symptoms, but God's mercy compelled me to drive myself to the hospital to receive care. I was surprised to learn that only 12 percent survive it. I'm still praising God!

This I know—transition is easier when you do it together. Those situations, and more between the lines, I have faced without Jeff.

There's a beloved line in a '70s song by Fleetwood Mac that I was sure Stevie Nicks must've written for me. It's about a landslide when we're afraid of life changing. And we question if we can handle the seasons even though time makes us bolder. And older.

I could have written a few sequels to the first book that I wrote ten years ago. We probably all could, because all of us have a book within us. Think of what has happened to you in the last 3,650 days. A lot can happen over a decade, but when change takes place radically and rapidly, it gets our attention in a new way.

And it did.

We never exit these trials the same way we enter. God will always meet us in a deeper way. Life can change in an instant and forever, but there will always be a next chapter. But knowing Him helps us turn the page with new perspective.

**We never exit these trials the same way we enter.
God will always meet us in a deeper way.**

Some of the seasons we move through are marked by the moments of joyful celebrations like weddings, births, and achievements, as well as times of grief such as death, loss, and hurt. Think of the many changes of seasons we experience in a lifetime. Some are sweet, some are hard—but every one of them will shape us. Which one has shaped you most?

And which one season would you choose to live in forever? Mine would be mama-hood, hands down. All cherished moments, even the teething and tantrums, bad dreams, and skinned knees, because there were always the *once upon a time* bedtime stories to end the day.

I can remember yesterday today, when my children took steps into the world without me. It all made sense out of the backstory.

But then in a nanosecond, home-sweet-nest became empty and I cried like they died. I would visit the museum of their room and smell the sweet scent of where they'd been in my mama-space—the safe place where I could say good night, and knew that it would be.

Blink, blink. Seasons quickly change. This is one of the great transitions in life for parents. My children are just about ready for AARP (true story), my grandchildren are grown and flown, and I stand in awe of seeing all of them in my little great-grandchild's laughter.

We get a little over two decades to get ready, but we never really do. And we know it's all about perspective, because we never really retire from the season of mama. We will always pray for the one who is just dwelling under a new roof. Lifetime prayers.

If you're a pre-nester and still have teenagers at home, hug the moment. If you're a post-nester, enjoy *you* and take solid steps to press deeper into the Father who is the One who mends the skinned heart of the mom of a fledgling.

And then, whisper to yourself, "This is simply a transition, a fresh season. You've done well."

> *I am not saying this because I am in need,*
> *for _____ has learned to be content*
> *whatever the circumstances.*
> *(from Philippians 4:11–12)*

even now

pause in the middle

What has been the hardest change in life for you?

14
when you haven't got a prayer

When we cannot pray as we would, it is good to pray as we can.
CHARLES SPURGEON

Charles Spurgeon had incredible oratory skills, but some of his quotes make my head hurt. I'm thinking this one means that in the times when we are so faint that we can only lie and breathe, then let our breath be prayer.

Prayer is our lifeline. Think of what it would be like if we couldn't ask our heavenly Father for protection, comfort, healing, provision, strength, and miracles—for our families, our friends, our nation, our strangers. To pray is the most powerful thing we can do for another. So, imagine if we couldn't pray.

I don't want to.

I think back to praying to a God I didn't know, when I was twelve years old, for a classmate not expected to live. And He heard and answered. What if I didn't? Would he have lived? Who knows the answer to either one, but this I do know: it mattered enough to be a lasting wonder to me for all of these decades.

That God heard me. *Me.*

I think back to the face down on the floor, face up to heaven, or face soaked with tears at the edge of a cornfield, praying for countless situations that I had no control over. It was prayer that talked me off the edge.

Have you come to a defeated place where sadness has stolen your words? You're running on prayer-empty and can't string one more holy syllable together to whisper a plea. I hear ya. And thankfully, so does the Holy Spirit who hears the language of our longing and gathers the groans to place before the Father.

When I was a new believer, I was drawn to stories of people in the Bible who knew what it was to cry out to God. They poured out a hurting heart, not in a lifeless scripted prayer but with raw holiness. I am still drawn to those stories, so I often visit the prayer lives of Hannah, David, Elijah, Paul, and so many others. Strange, how even those who demonstrated bulldog faith wrestled in prayer with petition and lament.

The way we perceive God influences the way we go before Him. If we see Him as a good and kind Father, we will pray differently than if we view Him as a distant deity hidden by clouds that doesn't give a rip.

I discovered gold while sitting at the prayerful bedside of my children and grandchildren, listening to their wonder that touches heaven purely by being real. Children are honest and humble, bold and expectant. I want to pray like a child.

Praying like a child reveals that it is in the sacred way God shows us who He is when we linger over a wildflower. We see more than the wildflower.

Yet there are the times when I've been the scattered soul, praying a distracted ritual "Christopher Robin prayer." I used to play a song for my older kids when they were young, recorded by Melanie, a hippie-era folk singer from the Woodstock days. She put a sweet tune to "Christopher Robin Is Saying His Prayers," inspired by a *Vespers* poem written by A. A. Milne, creator of the beloved Winnie the Pooh.

It captures the authenticity between the innocent lines as the "little boy kneels at the foot of his bed, droops on the little hands his little gold head. Hush, hush whisper who dares, Christopher Robin is saying his prayers."

> God bless Mummy, I know that's right.
> And wasn't it fun in the bath tonight?
> The cold's so cold, and the hot's so hot,
> Oh! God bless Daddy—I quite forgot.
> If I open my fingers just a little bit more,
> I can see Nanny's dressing gown on the door.
> It's a beautiful blue, but it hasn't got a hood.
> Oh! God bless Nanny and make her good.
> Mine has a hood and if I lie in bed,
> And put the hood right over my head,
> And I shut my eyes, and I curl up small,
> And nobody knows that I'm there at all.
> Oh! Thank you God, for a lovely day.
> And what was the other I wanted to say?
> I said "Bless Daddy," so what can it be?
> Now I remember. God bless me![1]

Have you noticed when we set our hearts to pray, the world pushes its way in? Instead of realizing we're before the throne of grace (the throne of grace!), we're noticing bathrobes on the door or a warm bath while asking scrambled blessings on loved ones. Suddenly, we have the urge to get up to feed the cat, load the laundry, and text Mom back immediately before she imagines the worst. Or maybe that's only my problem.

When we sit on the steps of our soul and appreciate what a privilege it is to carry everything to Him, it should slay us in absolute wonder.

When we sit on the steps of our soul and appreciate what a privilege it is to carry everything to Him, it should slay us in absolute wonder. I believe we get tangled in designing our prayers to be original and poetic, but maybe a simple prayer to Jesus through the Holy Spirit with ancient language is what we need most. Or maybe even a borrowed prayer.

Hannah taught me how to pray when my only prayers dripped down my face in desperation. She was a woman described as downhearted. Her story is in the book of 1 Samuel 1. She remained faithful and fervently poured out travailing prayer before the only One who could change the course of her life. She begged for a child. Hannah's testimony is that a sovereign God can and does reverse human circumstances. *Fervent* isn't an everyday word for today, but it's a good word. It means having a passionate intensity. Do you have an earnest intention to lift up the need that brings your heart down? Pray along with Hannah in 1 Samuel 2:1–10.

Hezekiah's prayer in Isaiah 38 has been my own. His prayer was a desperate appeal for deliverance when the prophet shared a diagnosis of terminal illness. Hezekiah reminded God of his faithfulness. God then mercifully extended his life for fifteen years. This was a prayer I called upon during my husband's hopeless diagnosis while in a coma. Pray with him in Isaiah 38:1–20.

And how grateful I was to pray along with Habakkuk in 3:2. How can this be a model for us to pray today? He is motivated by remembering what God has done in his life. Because he looks backward in reverence, he can lean forward in faith to say, "Lord, do it again." The prayer life of Habakkuk was central in bringing me through hard days with my baby son Geoff. Habakkuk 2:3—"Record the vision. . . . Though it tarries, wait for it; for it will certainly come, it will surely come" (NASB1995)—is the center square that holds my testimony quilt stitched together. It was what held me together and inspired me to begin journaling decades ago, as I looked backward while leaning forward.

Nehemiah's prayer life inspired me greatly while we were building our home with the help of our Bible study gang. We lost our home due to an overload of medical bills when my family was young. I read in the book of Nehemiah how he wept over the loss and destruction of Jerusalem. He had to rebuild. He not only prayed for restoration, he prayed with action. Our friends who met on Tuesday nights to study the Bible in an old farmhouse, came together as gifted laymen to form a construction crew. A mason, carpenter, plumber, and electrician all helped my husband build our home from foundation to roof.

This beautiful act of brotherhood blessed our family, our church, and our community to witness the only blueprint we followed: "The God of heaven Himself will prosper us. Therefore . . . arise and build" (Nehemiah 2:20).

And then there's Paul's powerful prayer life that I borrowed to pray as a mom during the prodigal years. A prodigal isn't simply a rebellious teen; it's just someone who needs to "come home." And don't we know many?

> I do not cease to give thanks for you, remembering you in my prayers, that the God of our Lord Jesus Christ, the Father of glory, may give you the Spirit of wisdom and of revelation in the knowledge of him, having the eyes of your hearts enlightened, that you may know what is the hope to which he has called you, what are the riches of his glorious inheritance in the saints, and what is the immeasurable greatness of his power toward us who believe, according to the working of his great might that he worked in Christ when he raised him from the dead and seated him at his right hand in the heavenly places, far above all rule and authority and power and dominion, and above every name that is named, not only in this age but also in the one to come. (Ephesians 1:16–21 ESV)

And the life-changing prayer in Colossians:

> For this reason we also, since the day we heard it, do not cease to pray for you, and to ask that you may be filled with the knowledge of His will in all wisdom and spiritual understanding; that you may walk worthy of the Lord, fully pleasing Him, being fruitful in every good work and increasing in the knowledge of God; strengthened with all might, according to His glorious power, for all patience and longsuffering with joy; giving thanks to the Father who has qualified us to be partakers of the inheritance of the saints in the light. (Colossians 1:9–12)

When our own prayers fall short in the middle of too much, the beauty of Scripture reminds us we don't need to depend on eloquence or strength, simply a heart tied to His.

I may not understand Spurgeon's quote, but I have the assurance to pray as I can.

In the same way, the Spirit helps us in our weakness. We do not know what we ought to pray for, but the Spirit himself intercedes for _____ through wordless groans.
(from Romans 8:26)

pause in the middle

If you had only one last prayer to offer, what would it be?

15
still yourself

Let us be silent, that we may hear the whisper of God.
RALPH WALDO EMERSON

When I was a little girl I was continually reminded to stop "fidgeting." This was back when we considered it normal to be bored. Today I'd be diagnosed with letters that stand for *not able to sit still.*

In elementary school, in between the instructions of "Sit still, Miss Rose," the teacher would have me wash the blackboards or "clap the erasers" (you probably have to be a *The Waltons* or *Little House on the Prairie* fan to get what that even is).

We used to visit my grandparents almost daily. Daily! If it went on longer than I could stand, I moved from one chair to another, shifting from one leg to another, while juggling knickknacks, hoping my dad would get the message that I wanted to *go*! But all movement would come to a stop with a quick reprimand from salty Irish Grandma Rose: "Still yourself, child. You must have bugs in your britches."

It's odd that I grew up so chill when I was such an itch of a kid. I guess the reason I outgrew it as an adult is because this life hasn't been a bit boring (if you've been reading).

We live in a busy, noisy world. If we are going to grow in our faith to have a deeper relationship with Jesus, we must be intentional to take time to be quiet before Him. To still our soul requires intention to listen for His voice, because the world has a voice too. Our Father speaks to us through His Word, through His people, and through our circumstances—within.

And if we don't listen, how can we hear?

There was a time when the only thing I thought I heard Him say was, "Don't do that!"

Most people would rather be doing something than doing nothing. A study about ten years ago found that people would rather push a button to receive an electric shock than to be in solitude for fifteen minutes, alone with their thoughts.[1] In a world of constant stimulation, we don't do well when forced to be s-t-i-l-l. It's so quiet! In the midst of persistent clamor and distraction, we forget what it is to just nestle into ourselves.

When I was a young and busy mom and homemaker, I was desperate for quiet. I hear from so many young moms who know exactly what that means. My granddaughter is a nursing mom to a busy, teething, crawling, chattery little son who expects her to be on duty in between being a wife, homemaker, and part-time NICU nurse. She is a mama who struggles for quiet time.

I love the example and heritage of Susannah Wesley, the mother of Charles and John (and seventeen others). An amazing lady of the late 1600s, she knew the secret of meeting with the Father in sacred privacy even while raising (and homeschooling) nineteen children! She couldn't find anywhere within her modest home to be alone with the Lord. Small wonder. So she pulled her apron over her head when she wanted her children to know it was time to leave her be still in the sanctuary of her heart.

I didn't have a Susannah-apron, so my prayer closet was the cornfield behind our home. I often wish I could return to the kitchen window, washing supper dishes and hearing the sweet sounds of children playing that made up my life back then. But children grow and husbands go to heaven—and now I can hear the dust settle.

So, seasons change. Listen to the silence.

I don't need to run to the solitude of a cornfield any longer, but I still do. For me, it will remain a holy of holies. And it has been in a vacant church in Bucks County where I rode a bicycle to speak a prayer for a young classmate to live. And it has also been in the cold hospital elevator, trying to hold on to sanity between floors as I left a loved one. Stillness is anywhere we drop to the knees of our heart to listen to God's heart.

Have you noticed how we sometimes over-prepare for a *splendid* isolation?

We seem to think that to have devotions we need a complete "stillness kit" made up of Bible, journal, coffee, an overstuffed comfy chair, and cue the cat to purr. Then everything hits the fan. The doorbell rings, the dog barks, the cat jumps out of our lap and spills coffee on the journal. Stillness over.

Then there are the times when all of it works—perfectly. And it becomes so still, the white noise reminds us we should throw the laundry in the dryer, unload the dishwasher, and clean a closet on the way.

I was raised with a "git 'er done" mentality and now live

in an anxiety culture where everyone begs to know what will happen next. It's a challenge to rest in the moment. We have to continually reframe spiritually and mentally. But once we learn the art of abiding on a daily basis, the time and place will always be there for secret intimacy, and it will become more second nature and part of who we are.

Over the years, I've learned that the secret to peace and confidence can be found in eight life-changing words: "Be still, and know that I am God" (Psalm 46:10 ESV).

Easy to memorize but not easy to remember. Write it down and put it at your desk at work, post it on the bathroom mirror, write it on your palm, tattoo it on your wrist, or stitch and hang over the fireplace. The original Hebrew word for *still* means relax, let go, cease, or withdraw, and it's hard to do when we're used to trying to control our kingdom.

All the truths we know about God's goodness can get rearranged when we are wondering why He is as still as we are asked to be. Even then, in the stillness He is moving. I emotionally transport myself back to a suffering child's bedside and countless hospital vigils for a dying husband—and I can honestly say that if I am *really* still, I can *really* know that He is *really* God. Otherwise, I couldn't be still.

I would have to run. And run.

When life is made up of the wild weight of all that and we don't have room left in our cluttered head, it has to be a deliberate practice to abide. Practice makes it grow, build, and morph. The *do* and the *be*. To be still is not a drive-by glance. When we linger, it will open our eyes to the bigness of God. How high and wise and sovereign deep that He can actually keep us in the times that are humanly impossible to *just let go.*

It is in those uncontrollable times, we must rehearse the I Am God who is the bread, light, gate, good shepherd, resurrection, and life, and is good to meet us in every unknown next. He is good when we get the devastating call in the middle of the night, in the middle of a broken relationship and the no-hope diagnosis, and even when the child we poured our life into decides to throw theirs away.

Even then.

Even now.

So still yourself for God to place His ear on your heart and hear it breaking. Lovely friend, there is no formula to tell another how to create the sacred space only you and God fit into. It's a desire that can't be found in a five-step formula, but can be found within three verses.

If we could paint the short Scripture of Psalm 131:1–3, it would be a portrait that shows true rest and abandonment:

> O Lord, my heart is not proud, nor my eyes haughty; nor do I involve myself in great matters, or in things too difficult for me. Surely I have composed and quieted my soul; like a weaned child resting against his mother, my soul is like a weaned child within me. (NASB)

This psalm isn't for the super-spiritual. It guides the one who simply needs to rehearse rest again and again. This psalm is for me. It reminds me of a beautiful snapshot of the sweet contentment of my great-grandbaby, Shepherd, as he rests safely on his mother. If you're a mom or a gramma and have held a child securely upon the breast while the other kids were fussing at your feet, then you know how the child close to your heartbeat rests in undisturbed composure. We need to get to the place of unshakable stillness where we can lean into the Father and feel His holy breath blow upon our hair amid the hush of the scramble.

> *Oh, _____, hope in the Lord*
> *from this time forth and forever.*
> *(from Psalm 131:3)*

pause in the middle

Do you make time for a personal retreat within your day? I hope you'll take a still moment now.

16
be the warrior

The enemy will not see you vanish into God's company without an effort to reclaim you.

C. S. LEWIS

If you're residing on my globe, you'll agree it's a war zone. In a hurting world of headlines, you may have noticed the lights growing more dim in an already dark place. Finding peace and courage in everyday life can be difficult in our present culture. Our thoughts go into overdrive when we think of what our world is facing and what it means for our children and grandchildren. Holding on to the hope we have in Jesus is the battle cry.

Half the battle is knowing that the enemy is real. One of Satan's clever deceptions is to make us believe that he doesn't exist or to blow him off as a Halloween myth. If demons weren't real, Jesus wouldn't have had to cast out so many.

Satan has an origin and he has a defeated end. So he's definitely real. He was beautifully created as an exalted angel who was then cast down to Eden. And you've heard the story.

He's smarter than you know. He's a word-twisting liar. Interestingly, the first question asked in the Bible wasn't spoken by God, but rather by Satan. He can take the form of whatever he likes. A snake was a good fit. So he slithered up to the first woman and hissed in her ear, "Did God really ssssay?"

He's been asking the same question since, because it worked in the garden. How many times has he asked you the same? Once you come out of the kingdom of darkness and into the kingdom of heaven, ready or not, it's war. Better learn how to fight.

As followers of Christ, it's up to us to be on guard. Satan isn't called crafty for nothing. I talk with women who say spiritual warfare is not something they hear much about in the church. Why is that? As Christian women, our heart's battle is to protect our home, marriage, and children in the day of reckless evil. The enemy of our soul is trying to take control of that precious territory. We have been a target since the garden because moms are the steward of home and hearth. Satan's warfare on women and her seed isn't his side job. It's his day (and night) job.

I've been around for quite a while—and a believer for more than half a while. Obviously, there has always been a struggle of good and evil in the world, but the intensity is far more evident today. There was a time when the words *spiritual warfare* caused some to roll their eyes. Not so much anymore. The evidence for evil in the world is not hard to see. The prophetic clock is ticking, and we have to be more serious than ever concerning the battle for our faith.

Actually, I experienced a few dark supernatural occurrences before I became a believer. I'll tell you about one. At a time when I was tangled up with a twisted circle of "friends" who were part of witchcraft, psychics, and gurus, among others that can take you down the same dark hole, my household was subject to quite a few strange events. Although a number of friends were into the occult, it was something I wanted no involvement in.

During one creepy episode, an acquaintance known to cast spells "gifted" me with a miniature decorative mask from the West Indies attached to a piece of black rawhide. Guessing it was a necklace? Not my best gift. It was hideous. I considered it a joke, at first. But, no joke, after a series of weird happenings, I couldn't get rid of it fast enough. As I was driving one night, I threw it out my car window onto the side of the highway. Turned out the very place I tossed it was the same stretch of road where my husband (at the time) had a horrific car accident a few weeks later.

I mention this strange incident because it was a dramatic point that helped me to see that there was more to what I didn't understand than what I understood. If you know what I mean. I didn't know what to make of it since I didn't believe in anything divine or evil back then. I was content to walk in ignorance based upon blind imitation. The enemy must love that. Satan's strategy may differ depending on whether someone is already a Christian or not, but the ultimate goal is always to keep people from experiencing the love of God:

> The god of this age has blinded the minds of unbelievers so that they cannot see the light of the gospel that displays the glory of Christ, who is the image of God. (2 Corinthians 4:4 NIV)

And Christians beware, if you look for a demon under every rock, chances are one might oblige you, so don't snoop in vain. Sometimes what we perceive as spiritual warfare may actually be God testing and refining us (see Psalm 66:10). Or it may be reaping what we have sown. Not every hardship in life is spiritual warfare. Jesus said we would face trouble in the world but He came to overcome. In warfare, our preoccupation shouldn't be with the devil, but with God. Only when we are submitted humbly and indwelt by His grace are we able to oppose the enemy of our soul with victory. That's why, simply put, "Therefore submit to God. Resist the devil and he will flee from you" (James 4:7).

Only when we are submitted humbly and indwelt by His grace are we able to oppose the enemy of our soul with victory.

We are wildly loved by a victorious Savior who fights for us and has left us His Word to use as a weapon. So many women have been deceived or know of someone who has been weighed down by the lies of the enemy. When marriages fall apart or kids fall away, we're convinced it must be because *we* failed and we're to blame for everything. We can be our best critic and place ourselves at the root of every struggle. When words like *not valuable*, *inadequate*, and *unforgiven* get written on our heart, we have to talk back. The only way to diffuse a lie is with the truth, so start believing and memorizing what God says about you.

Significant, treasured, forgiven, and *His.*

Today we can't let the enemy catch us half-dressed. Our battle attire is found in our prayer closet, and it equips us to go forward with bold determination in the full armor of

God. And when someone sees you standing firm in the rubble and comments on your royal wardrobe, simply say, "This old thing? My helmet of salvation, breastplate of righteousness, and girdle of truth? I've had it for years and it still fits!"

Our timeless ensemble goes well with a shield and a sword. And wondering what shoes match the outfit? Put on the sandals of peace and spread Jesus with every step you take.

Paul the apostle knew how to dress a girl for success in six easy steps:

> Stand therefore, having girded your waist with truth, having put on the breastplate of righteousness, and having shod your feet with the preparation of the gospel of peace; above all, taking the shield of faith with which you will be able to quench all the fiery darts of the wicked one. And take the helmet of salvation, and the sword of the Spirit, which is the word of God; praying always with all prayer and supplication in the Spirit, being watchful to this end with all perseverance and supplication for all the saints. (Ephesians 6:14–18)

When you hear a wicked whisper, fight like a Spirit-filled girl and wield the sword of the Spirit that says "it is written" and post it everywhere it'll stick. Remember, the Scriptures are so powerful, even the Son of God used them to battle His adversary.

As the Lord brings you to victory, ask Him what spoils of war He has for you to gather from what the enemy has been holding on to. Is it physical healing, salvation of loved ones, restoration in fractured relationships, or deliverance from what has been tormenting you? Remember, a new strength and anointing comes in victory that gives us greater power to overthrow our enemy in the battles that lie ahead. Be encouraged.

Be the warrior.

No weapon formed against _____ shall prosper, and every tongue that shall rise against you in judgment, you shall show to be wrong. This is the heritage of the servants of the Lord. This is the righteousness or the vindication which they obtain from me, says the Lord.
(from Isaiah 54:17)

pause in the middle

What spoils of war does God have for you to gather from what the enemy has been holding on to?

17
the caller is the keeper

If God sends us on strong paths, we are provided strong shoes.
CORRIE TEN BOOM

No matter what the journey holds, we can be assured we don't go it alone. Jesus didn't save us so we could flounder on our own. He who called us, keeps us.

I've been asked, "How do you know God is real?" My confident answer is, "I've experienced Him. *Someone* had to be watching over all this. I know I've needed more than me along the way."

This coming September will be my fiftieth birthday in Jesus. He chose me and asked me to choose Him. Glad I did, He's been a faithful Savior. The unknown was ahead, and reviewing my life, I could have never come from point A to almost point Z without His keeping power. *Never.*

The longer I live, the more I realize life is beyond human ability.

You probably know this one: persevering in faith doesn't rest on us. If we can't recognize our need for holy-keeping, we're in for a fall. We can't muster up faith by trying harder. Thankfully, we are gifted with a Spirit when we are called, to keep us.

Today, we hear of many who lose heart and abandon their faith for various reasons. I want to listen to them. I want to hear the answer to where they will find strength and hope if confronted with a terminal diagnosis or a world crisis, or when they have to hear "dust to dust" spoken over a loved one. Where will they find true peace, comfort, guidance, and joy if not in Jesus?

If you're there or have ever been there, hold tight to the One who will not let you go. If His hand can rescue us, He has a strong enough grip to keep us from the pull of the world. As we pray for ourselves or those we love, it's easy to think that the circumstances pressing in on all sides are strong enough to defeat us.

> Great is His faithfulness. His mercies begin afresh each morning. (Lamentations 3:25 NLT)

My prayer for you and for me is to live in that verse. As long as we can greet fresh mercy every morning, we can know we're being kept.

As long as we can greet fresh mercy every morning, we can know we're being kept.

God keeps us in many ways. Through His Word, through the Spirit, through His people. I'm grateful for those placed on my path who have helped me to walk strong. Surely you recall times when you were at your broken-most, and just before the clock struck too-late, you received a call or visit from a praying friend.

If you are at the raw end of the rope and wonder how you can continue when you have failed so often, fell too many times, and don't have the strength to keep on, please know, you have a nail-pierced hand and a watchful eye upon you.

Take heart, friend. You have a keeper of your soul who travels the journey with you as He did with those who sung Psalm 121 along the way . . .

> I lift up my eyes to the mountains—
> where does my help come from?
> My help comes from the LORD,
> the Maker of heaven and earth.
> He will not let your foot slip—
> he who watches over you will not slumber;
> indeed, he who watches over Israel
> will neither slumber nor sleep.
> The LORD watches over you—
> the LORD is your shade at your right hand;
> the sun will not harm you by day,
> nor the moon by night.
> The LORD will keep you from all harm—
> he will watch over your life;
> the LORD will watch over your coming and
>   going
> both now and forevermore.
> (NIV)

So, how can we prevent ourselves from taking the keeping power of God for granted? By imagining our lives without it.

even now

Fear not, for I am with _____;
be not dismayed, for I am your God.
I will strengthen you, I will help you,
I will uphold you with my righteous right hand.
(from Isaiah 41:10)

verna bowman

pause in the middle

In what ways has the Lord been traveling your journey with you?

18
soul mentoring

> *No one is more influential in your life than you are
> because no one talks to you as much as you talk to yourself.*
> PAUL DAVID TRIPP, *NEW MORNING MERCIES*

Would you believe you can make a difference in your emotional, spiritual, and physical well-being by talking to yourself? It matters how we coach ourselves through feelings of fear, anger, unforgiveness, and despair because those emotions can do a lot of damage to our soul. And we all have been touched by them.

Knowing how to encourage ourselves to secure healing and hope to meet the challenges we face today, and doing it, is renewing our mind.

I don't know how to do it without a Bible. Do you know another way? When you are overwhelmed, do you chat with your soul and give it a word to reboot? Think of the barrage of thoughts that go through your mind daily. I read that the average person has over six thousand thoughts a day and 75 percent are negative. And then we sleep a portion of the twenty-four hours, but how many thoughts while we sleep? If you're a mom, there are the overwhelming concerns over every kid you've ever had—always in the middle of the night. Thank God for the light of Jesus that leads us out of the darkness of our mind.

We need to give our mind a Sunday in which it ceases from work to simply restfully soak in the dew of heaven. Especially when we begin to tell ourselves that our prayers are simply noise banging on the holy ceiling and no one is answering.

We need to give our mind a Sunday in which it ceases from work to simply restfully soak in the dew of heaven.

Mind your mind.

Think about your day or your last week. How could it have been different if you reversed the negative by affirming yourself with a positive? The way to diffuse what is getting in the way of organic pure and noble thinking is a word that speaks back.

If the struggle is with fearful, anxious thoughts, we need to identify and cling to a word to strengthen during those times. Such as . . .

> The Lord is near. Do not be anxious about anything, but in every situation, by prayer and petition, with thanksgiving, present your requests to God. And the peace of God, which transcends all understanding, will guard your hearts and your minds in Christ Jesus. (Philippians 4:5–7)

A tremendous weight on our soul is unforgiveness. We've heard it before: "Forgiveness is a choice. Forgive as we have been forgiven. We must forgive and forget." All true, but depending on the depth of the wound that wrecks us, it can feel impossible to carry out. And it is, without the Holy Spirit of God to do it through us.

Forgiveness has been a repeated theme in my life. Big things, unforgettable things. And I learned a long time ago, forgiving someone doesn't bring an instant memory lapse. But if we aren't forgetting, we're busy remembering. If we beat ourselves up over bad memories, it will only add to the hurt.

Forgiveness mysteriously brings healing to our souls. It takes obedience to choose to forgive in the moment while waiting for our heart to catch up. But it takes faith to allow it to be settled in the courts of heaven. Maybe you have heard it said, "Unforgiveness is like drinking poison and waiting for the other person to die." You may also have heard, "Forgiveness is the fragrance the violet sheds on the heel that has crushed it."

Maybe your self-talk has told you, "I'll never get over this. I'll never trust anyone again. God will only disappoint me. I wouldn't be going through this if I was a better Christian."

Lies.

Throughout the long years when I was tempted to argue with my journal, I have had to preach *it is absolutely okay with my soul* in order to believe it in times of deep despair. King David spoke to his soul continually all throughout the Psalms. I love saints of old who carry lamps of the Word into our dark places.

Scripture mentors our soul. And what has talked me off the ledge is a particular Bible. Not just any Bible. I have a Bible that is different from *anyone* else's. The sister sitting next to me may think she's holding the same book, even the same version, but it isn't the same as my tear-stained, margin-marked book of chronicled life where heaven met the page. It isn't the same *as mine*. My God met me in every holy syllable to direct and comfort, chastise and grow me — all between the battered leather covers of what I fondly refer to as my "Transplant Bible." A collection of sixty-six books just like yours, but this one holds the Voice that spoke personally through each one throughout a decades-long journey. Manna scribed in the margins.

Many psalms have encouraged my heart through the *from so far there to so far here* journey. This is only one, Psalm 103. I don't know what kind of day David was having when he jotted these honest words, but I'm pretty sure it was a time when he was overwhelmed with life. Like us. He begins the psalm by telling his soul to bless the Lord.

> Bless the LORD, O my soul;
> And all that is within me, bless His holy
>   name!
> Bless the LORD, O my soul,
> And forget not all His benefits:
> Who forgives all your iniquities,
> Who heals all your diseases,
> Who redeems your life from destruction,
> Who crowns you with lovingkindness and
>   tender mercies,
> Who satisfies your mouth with good things,
> So that your youth is renewed like the eagle's.
> (vv. 1–5)

The beautiful benefits of the Lord stuffed into five verses. He forgives, heals, redeems, crowns, satisfies, and renews. We can encourage ourselves to last a lifetime in just this passage. David doesn't specifically tell us how to encourage ourselves in the Lord, but it's easy to see it is by remembering who God is and how He can be trusted.

David's story is told in the book of 1 Samuel and wrapped up in one verse: "David was deeply distressed . . . but [he] encouraged himself in the Lord his God" (30:6 ESV).

He didn't have a training program for shepherd boys in how to get from pasture to palace while hiding in a cave from a maniac king or taking down a giant in the middle of his story. What he had was complete dependence on the Sovereign, and he remained a man after God's own heart. Even a man after God's own heart succumbed to the emotions that discourage our soul.

There isn't a human dwelling on this planet, then or now, who isn't acquainted with troubles. Sorrow can take root in our head. So, there's nothing new under the sun — not for David, not for us. That's why he chose to mentor himself and rehearse the good to silence the bad.

May we learn from him.

Whatever is true, whatever is noble, whatever is right, whatever is pure, whatever is lovely, whatever is admirable — if anything is excellent or praiseworthy — dwell on such things, _____.
(from Philippians 4:8)

pause in the middle

What good can you rehearse to silence the bad?

19
it is well

Take away the stone.
JESUS

A dead man was on the other side of the stone. Lazarus. Dead enough to stink.

A man pronounced brain dead was on the other side of the hospital door. My husband.

And they lived. Both scenes surpass sound reasoning, I know.

How can we, as finite-thinking humans, believe there can be hope in either situation? This must be the wildly ridiculous place where we choose to *just* believe or *still* believe. The truth is not always what I expect it to be, because faith and logic seem to contradict each other, but one transcends the other in the few stories that have changed my expectations.

And I've told you a few, but not in this way.

Logic says, "A child who has only two percent kidney function at birth is not expected to live." The reality: Our newborn son was thirty minutes from stillbirth. Despite countless negative reports, he survived in neonatal intensive care for months. Throughout his life, despite negative reports, he survived multiple transplants. Faith says, "With God all things are possible" (Matthew 19:26 NIV).

Faith says, "With God all things are possible."

Logic says, "A young man in a near-fatal car wreck with multiple severed internal organs is not expected to live. A foot crushed to powdered bone and near to needing amputation cannot be used to walk again. A bladder that has been shot apart by traumatic impact that cannot be surgically repaired after several attempts can no longer function." The reality: Airlifted to a trauma center, admitted as an unrecognizable John Doe, and three teams of doctors tried to save our son. After remaining for months in the ICU, it seemed necessary to have him transferred to Duke University or simply sent to a nursing home at twenty-six years old. Thankfully, that didn't happen. After months of rehabilitation and an extremely difficult recovery, he survived. And walked again. Faith says, "Trust in the LORD with all your heart, and lean not on your own understanding; in all your ways acknowledge Him, and He shall direct your paths" (Proverbs 3:5–6).

Logic says, "The one who is comatose with minimal brain function after suffering cardiac arrest and multiple strokes is not expected to survive. If he lives, he won't want to, considering quality of life." The reality: Following a lengthy process of therapy and rehabilitation to regain a somewhat normal life, he lived another fifteen years. Faith says, "I love the LORD, because He hears my voice and my supplications. Because He has inclined His ear to me, therefore I shall call upon Him as long as I live" (Psalm 116:1–2 NASB1995).

Logic says, "When one lung is perforated and the other is torn wide open, it can be fatal, because we cannot survive without air." The reality: My eighteen-month-old son Shane was rushed to the hospital with epiglottitis, a condition that blocks the flow of air to the lungs, causing sudden death. Since it's rare, there were only four cases that year in the entire county. Medical staff inserted the wrong size trach and it resulted in a code blue. A local pastor heard of the situation and came to the intensive care unit to pray over my child. He was one of the first to show me to believe in what faith says.

Logic says, "With head and neck cancer at this stage, there isn't much hope." The reality: After surgeries and radiation the situation looked worse than the prognosis for my oldest son, Tom. It was a time when faith says, "I believe, Lord. Help my unbelief" (Mark 9:24).

In the critical times when we are faced with stop-you-in-your-tracks events, ordinarily all we can see are scenes without hope. Our reality needs to be that nothing is too difficult for God, even in these times. But we know it's just not that simple. As I'm writing this tonight, a news alert has come on all stations of a medical jet plane crash in the crowded residential community of Philadelphia, just days after the tragic crash in the Potomac near to the Capitol. None survived in either one. Viewing God through the lens of this kind of trauma is complicated.

When logic and faith collide, do we *just* believe or do we *continue to* believe?

Sometimes the stone isn't rolled away. We don't understand why some situations turn out one way and others don't turn out at all. I know, because we have many yet-to-be-answered prayers in our family. I guess the real question is not "Why does God heal some and not others?" but rather "Why is anyone healed at all?"

We can't explain sovereignty, so don't try. And if we're honest, it can't always be well with our soul. Even when we're singing that it is.

But it's what we do. When we're in church, we sing. The person on the right, the one on the left, all together now, "Whatever my lot, thou hast taught me to say, it is well, it is well with my soul."[1] In between the lines, so many must want to shout, "But it's not, Lord! It's not well with my soul right now. And I wonder if it ever will be again."

You and I aren't the only ones who have felt this way. If the books of Job and Psalms teach us anything, it's that it's okay to lament. There are promises we need to hold on to when it is not well with our soul. Real faith is not always what we make it sound like—a pithy platitude or quick-fix verse when our world is falling apart. It's more honest than that.

I'm grateful for beautiful hymns like "It Is Well with My Soul." The lyrics of lament resonate through our humanity to tell the story that despite trials we can cling to abiding peace. If this song was written by someone who skipped through life, it wouldn't mean the same thing.

The one who penned the touching words, Horatio Spafford, is one who experienced life-altering tragedy when he lost everything. He lost his home in a fire, he lost a son, and later he lost four daughters (and almost his wife) in a shipwreck.

It is difficult to place ourselves in that kind of Job-like sorrow, but I'm certain there have been times for you also, when you stood stunned and silent in the wreckage. And if you're there now, I encourage you to find a life verse to hold on to—one Scripture that is like a personal touchstone in your faith journey and speaks into your life like no other. I hope you have one. If not, use mine:

> I would have lost heart [or fainted], unless I had believed that I would see the goodness of the LORD in the land of the living. (Psalm 27:13)

The fullness of the fourteen verses in Psalm 27 has taught me to grieve well and to believe well. It is a psalm of fearless trust that grows within us during dark times. Within its healing words is peace that passes our understanding to see the goodness of God no matter how dark the night becomes—even when we feel like we're collapsing under the affliction. Never give up your confidence in God's goodness and faithfulness to you. Please.

And then may we say (and sing!), "It is well with my soul"—and know that it's true.

> *Come see what our God has done, and what awesome miracles He performs for you, _____.*
> *(from Psalm 66:5)*

pause in the middle

What does it mean to you to "grieve well and believe well"?

20
yet...i will

Yet I will rejoice in the LORD, I will joy in the God of my salvation.
HABAKKUK 3:18 KJV

It all runs together but never runs out. The Word, I mean. It blends and builds and brings life to dead places. We're in the book of 1 Samuel on Thursday mornings in our Precept class, walking through the life of David as he triumphs and trips. I studied this book over twenty years ago, and yet it fits even more so today.

I love David and his realness; he taught me the importance of journaling.

At the moment, I'm reading the book of Habakkuk in the Old Testament, written by an ancient prophet who could've written this book after the evening news last night. Unearthing the gold in aged texts can open our eyes wide to the day. You may have noticed that we're living the Bible right now; we only have to check the page we're on.

This short book, just three chapters, is overflowing with

lessons for the moment. The perplexed prophet was weighed down with the frustration of his day when his land was invaded by the enemy. It seemed as though God was not doing anything about it. Sound familiar?

So, he poured his heart out before God with *a why and how long*, like we tend to do when our world seems to have been invaded by the enemy. Good has become wrong. Everything is okay and nothing is okay. And we're frustrated like Hab. So, there's that.

But *this* is what he did. He got honest: "How long, O LORD, will I call for help, and you will not hear?" (1:2 NASB1995). But God did answer: "Look among the nations . . . because I am doing something in your days—You would not believe if you were told" (v. 5 NASB1995). He believed and he waited and he trusted and he wrote it down. A progression that will never let you down. A chat and a journal between a real man and a real God.

I love Habakkuk and his realness; he taught me the importance of journaling.

Early on in my faith, I leaned on a particular verse in the book of Habakkuk when things looked hopeless in my life. So, it's stitched tight into the center square of my treasured testimony quilt:

> This word holds it together,
> I will stand on my guard post . . .
> And I will keep watch to see what He will
>   speak to me. . . .
> "Record the vision
> And inscribe it on tablets,
> That the one who reads it may run.
> "For the vision is yet for the appointed time;

It hastens toward the goal and it will not fail.
Though it tarries, wait for it;
For it will certainly come, it will not delay."
(Habakkuk 2:1–3 NASB1995)

It reminds me of how this verse is real for you and for me, that we can have a holy composure and a sacred joy, no matter our circumstances. If we *remember* as we write it down to have it *reinforced* in our heart, we can *rejoice* and *rest* in the truth despite our circumstances.

If we *remember* as we write it down to have it *reinforced* in our heart, we can *rejoice* and *rest* in the truth despite our circumstances.

The bittersweet story that begins with a complaint ends with composure. Ours can also.

> Though the fig tree should not blossom
> And there be no fruit on the vines,
> Though the yield of the olive should fail
> And the fields produce no food,
> Though the flock should be cut off from
>   the fold
> And there be no cattle in the stalls,
> Yet I will exult in the LORD,
> I will rejoice in the God of my salvation.
> (Habakkuk 3:17–18 NASB1995)

May we unearth the gold contained in the small books that remind us to cling to wild faith.
Even now.

even now

Look among the nations, _____,
because I am doing something in your days —
You would not believe if you were told.
(from Habakkuk 1:5)

verna bowman

pause in the middle

What bittersweet story of yours began with a complaint and ended with composure?

epilogue

epilogue

21
if you had a remembrance book

Fill your paper with the breathings of your heart.
WILLIAM WORDSWORTH

I remember the first time I met my husband. (Well, actually "remet" him, since I'd known him through friends of my first husband but hadn't seen him in about six years). It was love at first wink. I remember it in part, because I'm depending on my memory, and I wish I would have written my heart down on paper in that tender moment.

How well do you remember what you were feeling during a significant time in life—or even in this past week? You may have noticed cognitive recall only goes so far and that rich details can fade with time. This is why I journal. Ink doesn't forget. We're wired to remember, but only as black-and-white events. When we write it down, the things we thought we wouldn't forget somehow become Technicolor because we notice how God worked in between the lines.

When we write it down, the things we thought we wouldn't forget somehow become Technicolor because we notice how God worked in between the lines.

But maybe you don't like to write. Maybe you don't have time. Maybe you don't think you have anything to write about. Pen-in-hand journaling may seem like a bygone sentiment, but it is a beautiful act of remembrance to grow our faith. So don't say no just yet.

My desire to write was sparked by dear old Miss Neely, a prim spinster schoolmarm who seemed a thousand years old. She was my favorite teacher in grade school, back in the quaint age of "reading, writing, and 'rithmetic"—though I never cared about the last one. Miss Neely wore stockings with a seam that went up the back of her bone-thin legs. The silver-rimmed spectacles were balanced on her nose to sit right above a set of false teeth that clicked with every syllable as she read *The Five Little Peppers* during story time. And I've grown up to love all things *words*.

So ever since I've been able to string sentences together, I have recaptured life with a pen. There is a line from the beginning of a *Little House on the Prairie* episode where Laura says, "If I had a remembrance book, I would write about . . ."[1] She wrote about everything that mattered, because everything does.

I have too. For over four decades I have faithfully kept a journal. Reams filled with archived growth and failure, trusted secrets and family life, and a record of each breath and beat that is a memorial to God's goodness throughout it all. And why?

Because journaling is the art of remembering. It's a theme that runs throughout the Bible, especially the book of Psalms. David penned at least seventy-five describing a man after God's own heart within his psalming-journal. The raw honesty uncovers his emotional world as he pours a mix of passion, praise, fear, trust, and despair all over the page.

I began journaling around the time my fourth baby was born with an illness and nothing made sense any longer. Sitting on an old wooden swing hanging from a listening tree, I spoke up through the leaves hoping Someone would hear. I waited with a Bible and an old composition book for words to come that would help me see farther than *then*. There is something about chatting with Deity and writing it down that clears things up. Since that time, scribing life in a remembrance book has taught me to wait well.

The wonder of faith-journaling is that it's not about jotting down a brain dump, but about searching the depths to discover more of God and more of ourselves. When I feel like I'm sitting on that old wooden swing once again, I spread the entries open to the binding to read mercy to the edge of every page. You see, it isn't just reflecting on the past; it's creating a way to *remember forward* with hope and courage.

If He was there then, He'll be here now.

Even now.

There are times my journal is nothing more than a tattered scrap recklessly scribbled at a traffic light or jots on a napkin transcribed later into a treasured keepsake. Mostly, I want it to be in the sweet Selah pause-and-ponder times when I come quietly before the Lord to write thoughts of His greatness and have His voice fill in the white space.

Your story matters. I am convinced more than ever that our children and theirs need to know what we believe and why. So, "tell the old, old story, the unseen things in glory"[2] so they will learn to trust Jesus and have hope in a world made up of change and compromise. I realize that my grandchildren who are now in their twenties and thirties have never known a world without the threat or fear from the aftermath of 9/11.

> Tell your children of it, and let your children tell their children, and their children another generation.
> (Joel 1:3 ESV)

Also, the stories of those who went before us matter. Maybe you are fortunate enough to have an old diary of an ancestor. It would be for me like discovering gold if my grandmother would have kept a journal. I would love to read the century-old life of the girl who lived from Grover Cleveland until John F. Kennedy was assassinated. To see her blush between the vows when she married my grandfather at age fourteen. To feel her hopes when she was having all of her babies. To read her heart through world wars and more wars when four of her sons were serving.

Some words blow away in the wind of the day, but others need to be preserved on parchment as priceless jewels that leave a costly heritage to the next generation. It may be the legacy of hope and courage that you can leave for another.

Many people are hesitant to keep a journal because they don't want anyone to read their private thoughts someday. Private thoughts and specific names can easily be blotted out with a thick black marker. So don't waste your writing. It can be an heirloom of your faith.

Here are some benefits of keeping a journal:

- Keeps a record of your personal journey
- Provides a tangible account of God's blessings and builds your faith
- Allows you to slow down and meditate on Scripture
- Is a keeping place for inspirational quotes, sermons, and reflections
- Clarifies the reality of your life story
- Helps you pay attention to God and notice the holy in the ordinary
- Helps put feelings into words and words into feelings
- Records your growth and sanctification
- Chronicles and preserves His faithfulness

If you wonder whether anything can be significantly recorded about the fruit of your life, write it down and read it. For example . . .

- Describe what is different today than a year ago that you are grateful for.
- Write a *Dear Younger Me* letter.
- Copy a meaningful prayer from Scripture in your handwriting.
- Share a secret with your Father.
- Keep a *This week, I was most blessed by* . . . journal.

> *Preserve your memories, keep them well,*
> *what you forget you can never retell.*
> LOUISA MAY ALCOTT, *LITTLE WOMEN*

even now

pause in the middle

Make a list of the things you'd like to write about.

22
embrace your story

*Miracles are a retelling in small letters of the
very same story which is written across the whole world
in letters too large for some of us to see.*
C. S. LEWIS, *GOD IN THE DOCK*

I remember the exact day and divine instant when mercy met me in the middle of the madness. It was when I went to a church service and was saved by way of a child's hand.

If I ran into my unredeemed self that you first met in the beginning of these pages, I would ask her if she ever expected to meet the redeemed me. Did I leave her in the dust, or did I learn from her?

I learned so much from that much-younger me. If I could shout across the years, I would tell her she was braver than I knew.

It took some time for me to share my story because I didn't know it until I read it in my first book, *Crumbs Along the Broken Path*. I didn't want anyone to know that me. When we come out of hiding, there is something far more beautiful than we can understand when we take time to visit ourselves.

Don't ever think your story is unimportant. It could change someone's life and help someone survive what you have already gone through. I think of the countless books I've read that helped me along the way. A book that I had to read twice to believe it was written by somebody else, *As Silver Refined* by Kay Arthur, polished my soul. Sometimes a story written by another can seem like it's ours.

Would you praise God for your story if you knew it before you lived it? *Probably not* is my honest answer. I'm sure, if we could rewind life, we wouldn't want to. But I now know I wouldn't trade what I have experienced that has brought me so near to God.

We need to reason with our story, no matter how it reads, so we can give thanks for it.

Are you one of the many who are reluctant to share your story because you feel others will look down on you? Even if it's R-rated, it is a beautiful offering to the Father. Sharing our faith story isn't about trying to change the way others think; it's about changing the way they hope.

Sharing our faith story isn't about trying to change the way others think; it's about changing the way they hope.

What if Anne Frank, who told about her family in hiding during the Holocaust, would have kept her story to herself? Or if Corrie ten Boom would not have shared how she found hope in a concentration camp? Most of us don't have stories like that to share, but ours are valid and God-given to reach within the sphere of our influence. They are needed.

And what if the worst chapters of our life are the ones that tell the victories?

All of us have unmet challenges and many that we have already come through. It amazes me how we over-dramatize or compare to the stories of others when ours is the best. The unique and custom-designed holy biography written for only you! Why try to edit God?

I hope we're learning together that in order to embrace our past and present story, we have to rest in the Lord, remain in His Word, and rely on His Spirit to be able to give praise in the *even now* of it.

I don't know the plans He has for you, friend. But I encourage you to own your story and live it bravely. And then tell it. Our testimony is the jewel of our story.

We all have the same testimony with a different before, how, and after, but if you are a follower of Jesus, Psalm 107 tells your story and mine in just a few lines:

> Oh give thanks to the LORD, for He is good,
> For His lovingkindness is everlasting.
> Let the redeemed of the LORD say so. . . .
> They stumbled and there was none to help.
> Then they cried out to the LORD in their
>   trouble;
> He saved them out of their distresses.
> (vv. 1–2, 12–13 NASB1995)

If I were to choose a title for my story, it would be "Unwilted." I had to look this up since I didn't think it was a word. But *Merriam-Webster* lists the meaning as "not wilted."[1] Seriously.

So, if I could chat with you in the garden once again, Grandma Rose, I hope you would agree that this one word tells my story well, since you spoke the words that I haven't forgotten:

> *Flowers tell a story ~*
> *Some remain tall and stately and can face hard seasons.*
> *Some don't hold up, they get withered and wilted by life.*
> *You need to decide which one you will be, Verna Rose.*

I may have decided right then and there to be the one who remains the unwilted rose that, even when its head is lowered by life and appears wilted, will continue to believe that God is the holy water and the dew. Then when the time comes for it to lose life, it will be pressed inside a book and be forever preserved.

> *Then _____ cried out to the Lord*
> *in her trouble, and He saved her out of her distresses.*
> *(from Psalm 107:13)*

verna bowman

pause in the middle

So, what is your story? And what would the title be?

23
thus far

> *Hitherto hath the* LORD *helped us.*
> 1 SAMUEL 7:12 KJV

Life unfolds one wrinkle at a time, one story at a time. Each line and each story reassures me of God's steadfastness because *hitherto hath the Lord helped us*. Beautiful ancient words.

They come from the story of how the Lord delivered the Israelites when they were facing desperate times. As a tangible reminder of God's goodness, Samuel took a stone and named it Ebenezer, which means "thus far the Lord has helped." It sounds like it points backward, but if we take an aerial view of our life, it points forward because we still have farther to tread. More trials, more joys, more lessons.

I have stones. My journals.

So, we're at a place called *here*. Somewhere in the middle of the backward and the forward. What am I to do with the remaining? And what about you? I would love for you to review you, to survey life and what it has whittled you into.

I mentioned at the beginning of this book the faraway land I lived in, in my head before I fell head over heels in love with my Savior. One book cannot contain the wondrous work of God in my life. I've made a meager attempt to share how the God of heaven came near to show me how real He is. After three score and seven years of growing and knowing, I know I need more growing.

What do I tell those who have asked me how to make faith *real*? I don't know how to string the words together to make another person understand. Just, open your Bible and find Him waiting for you with wild love.

This book has been a feeble offering to express my gratitude for a faithful Father who came looking for a reckless teenager who thumbed her nose, a semi-reckless adult who did it twice, and took me for His bride to make me wholly His. You may have had a different path than I did. I hope you have. But if you have skipped blissfully through life with not a problem you can think of, thus far the Lord has helped you . . . too.

A new journal tells me another year is before me. To fill to the margin, all that Jesus is. Many hard changes have taken place in the world in the past five years since I began the first page of this manuscript. Yet, there are things in my personal world that have not changed at all—and I wish and I beg that they do.

I'm thankful it's taken this long. It's been a long and hard four-plus years, so it proves the point of needing to cling to wild faith. God's keeping power is the driving force to push against closed doors with holy audacity. And we will continue to do so.

So, where do we go from here? I pray I will remain steadfast even when I feel as though my faith is about to fold like a cheap tent. The word *steadfast* is a very spiritual word.

It means to be immovable, firmly fixed. Someone who is steadfast knows what they know and they walk in it.

I want to be her.

Someone who is steadfast knows what they know and they walk in it. I want to be her.

Every one of us has a story—differently the same. I have experienced a lot of life and a lot of God. And I have experienced miracles, undoubtedly. But through it all, the miracle has been getting through the middle of each story.

Whether I look back or beyond, Father God has brought our family through times that only God could bring us through. I've wondered how different I would be had I not had this story as the backdrop of my life. Not one chapter was written in vain.

No matter the stage of life that we are experiencing at the moment, may we claim the riches and create a *thus far* list. Make a list, just off the top of your heart, of the times when the Lord has helped you—answered a prayer of provision, offered comfort in a time of grieving, gave direction when you were uncertain, brought healing in a time of sickness or brokenness. The list will be endless. I know mine is.

And I assure you it will strengthen your faith and deep love.

Even now.

last thoughts

Hi. I'm so glad we got to spend time together.
I'm Verna. A passionate follower of Christ. A mom to Sherise and Scott, Tom, Shane, and Geoff. A gramma to Japheth and Rachel, Joah, Taleh and Christopher, Brianna and Logan, and Avery. And a great-gramma to Shepherd James. My beautiful family. I'm a widow missing Jeff. And a cat-mom to Glory.

I've worked in the medical community for over thirty years. I'm part of a loving church family at Immanuel Leidy's Church. And I'm grateful to have served in ministry to women for over thirty-five years. Also grateful to be part of Precept Bible Studies alongside the dearest Jesus-lovin' ones who have faithfully walked me through the hard middle. I love all things writing—authoring, blogging, journaling. And I love to tell the story as a conference speaker.

I wrote this book as an answer to a question I have been asked many times: How could a faithless rebel be so far away and over time gather enough faith to remain in the *even now* middle? The answer is, at the cross.

I've been lost and found and sold-out for Jesus, but kept seeking—daily. I will never stop wanting to learn what I think I already have.

The common thread that ties each of the chapters in this book together is Psalm 27:13:

> I would have despaired unless I had believed that I would see the goodness of the Lord in the land of the living. (NASB1995).

The greatest lesson we can learn in the wait of the devastatingly beautiful middle is to believe to see, for we may never get to the place He wants us if He were an instant God.

So, dear you, believe to see even now, no matter what you're looking at in the hard moment. Look for Him every day. Sit still. Listen and let Him get a word in edgewise. And you will be swept off your feet in love. To remain.

Even now.

notes

5. i don't remember me

1. Lewis Carroll, *Alice's Adventures in Wonderland* (London: Macmillan and Co., 1920), 58.

11. what if one line could tell your story?

1. *America's Got Talent*, season 16, episode 2, directed by Russell Norman, aired June 8, 2021 on NBC.
2. Jane Marczewski (@_nightbirde), "You can't wait until life isn't hard anymore before you decide to be happy," X, June 9, 2021, https://x.com/_nightbirde/status/1402495585693974529?.

14. when you haven't got a prayer

1. A. A. Milne, *Vespers*, https://www.worldprayers.org/archive/prayers/celebrations/little_boy_kneels_at_the.html.

15. still yourself

1. Nadia Whitehead, "We would rather be electrically shocked than left alone with our thoughts," Science.org, July 3, 2014, https://www.science.org/content/article/people-would-rather-be-electrically-shocked-left-alone-their-thoughts.

19. it is well

1. Horatio Spafford, "It Is Well with My Soul" (1876), (United Methodist Publishing House: *The United Methodist Hymnal*, 1989), no. 377.

notes

21. if you had a remembrance book

1. *Little House on the Prairie*, season 6, episode 1, "Back to School (Part I)," directed by Michael Landon, written by Blanche Hanalis, Laura Ingalls Wilder, and Michael Landon, aired September 17, 1979 on NBC.
2. Katherine Hankey, "I Love to Tell the Story" (1868), (United Methodist Publishing House: *The United Methodist Hymnal*, 1989), no. 156.

22. embrace your story

1. Merriam-Webster.com Dictionary, s.v. "unwilted," accessed February 28, 2025, https://www.merriam-webster.com/dictionary/unwilted.

acknowledgments

Ever grateful~

In the beginning, God knew me and you. I'm glad we found one another in these pages.

To the faithful ~ you know who you are.

To my dear family who taught me how to cling to faith and not release the grip. Special gratitude to daughter Sherise who spoke to me before she could talk.

To my critique gals who tightened, refined, and prayed this book into print.

And a huge ever-grateful to Christy Distler and Hannah Linder who made it all work.

In memory of Jeff, who changed my story.

about the author

VERNA BOWMAN is an author, a conference speaker, and a blogger at *Encouraging Women One Story at a Time*. Serving for over thirty-five years in various roles of ministry leadership has given her insight to and understanding of the needs of women today. Her mission is to inspire others to a deeper faith through God's Word and by sharing personal stories of His faithfulness.

Her story has been featured on *The 700 Club* and through countless articles published in *Guideposts*, *Women's Day*, *Power for Living*, *A Cup of Comfort Devotional* (Threads of Encouragement series), *Chicken Soup for the Soul*, *CBN*, and *INSP*. She is also the author of *Crumbs Along the Broken Path* and *Gathering Seeds of Encouragement*.

Verna is a widow, a proud mom to four, and a proud

gramma to more. She and her family live in Pennsylvania, and she continues to work in the medical community. For information on her ministry, visit www.vernabowman.com.

www.ingramcontent.com/pod-product-compliance
Lightning Source LLC
Chambersburg PA
CBHW011550070526
44585CB00023B/2526